Arizona Diamondbacks 2021

A Baseball Companion

Edited by Steven Goldman and Bret Sayre

Baseball Prospectus

Craig Brown, Associate Editor
Robert Au, Harry Pavlidis and Amy Pircher, Statistics Editors

Copyright © 2021 by DIY Baseball, LLC.
All rights reserved

This book or any part thereof may not be reproduced or transmitted in any form or by any means, electronic or mechanical, including photocopying, recording, or by any information storage and retrieval system, without permission in writing from the publisher.

Limit of Liability/Disclaimer of Warranty: While the publisher and the author have used their best efforts in preparing this book, they make no representations or warranties with respect to the accuracy or completeness of the contents of this book and specifically disclaim any implied warranties of merchantability or fitness for a particular purpose. No warranty may be created or extended by sales representatives or written sales materials. The advice and strategies contained herein may not be suitable for your situation. You should consult with a professional where appropriate. Neither the publisher nor the author shall be liable for any loss of profit or any other commercial damages, including but not limited to special, incidental, consequential, or other damages.

Library of Congress Cataloging-in-Publication Data:
paperback
ISBN-13: 978-1-950716-25-8

Project Credits
Cover Design: Ginny Searle
Interior Design and Production: Amy Pircher, Robert Au
Layout: Amy Pircher, Robert Au

Baseball icon courtesy of Uberux, from https://www.shareicon.net/author/uberux

Ballpark diagram courtesy of Lou Spirito/THIRTY81 Project, https://thirty81project.com/

Manufactured in the United States of America
10 9 8 7 6 5 4 3 2 1

Table of Contents

Statistical Introduction v

Part 1: Team Analysis
Performance Graphs 3
2020 Team Performance 4
2021 Team Projections 5
Team Personnel 6
Chase Field Stats 7
Diamondbacks Team Analysis 9

Part 2: Player Analysis
Diamondbacks Player Analysis 16
Diamondbacks Prospects 87

Part 3: Featured Articles
Diamondbacks All-Time Top 10 Players 101
   by Steven Goldman

A Taxonomy of 2020 Abnormalities 109
   by Rob Mains

Tranches of WAR 115
   by Russell A. Carleton

Secondhand Sport 121
   by Patrick Dubuque

Steve Dalkowski Dreaming 125
   by Steven Goldman

A Reward For A Functioning Society 129
   by Cory Frontin and Craig Goldstein

Index of Names 133

Statistical Introduction

Sports are, fundamentally, a blend of athletic endeavor and storytelling. Baseball, like any other sport, tells its stories in so many ways: in the arc of a game from the stands or a season from the box scores, in photos, or even in numbers. At Baseball Prospectus, we understand that statistics don't replace observation or any of baseball's stories, but complement everything else that makes the game so much fun.

What stats help us with is with patterns and precision, variance and value. This book can help you learn things you may not see from watching a game or hundred, whether it's the path of a career over time or the breadth of the entire MLB. We'd also never ask you to choose between our numbers and the experience of viewing a game from the cheap seats or the comfort of your home; our publication combines running the numbers with observations and wisdom from some of the brightest minds we can find. But if you *do* want to learn more about the numbers beyond what's on the backs of player jerseys, let us help explain.

Offense

We've revised our methodology for determining batting value. Long-time readers of the book will notice that we've retired True Average in favor of a new metric: Deserved Runs Created Plus (DRC+). Developed by Jonathan Judge and our stats team, this statistic measures everything a player does at the plate–reaching base, hitting for power, making outs, and moving runners over–and puts it on a scale where 100 equals league-average performance. A DRC+ of 150 is terrific, a DRC+ of 100 is average and a DRC+ of 75 means you better be an excellent defender.

DRC+ also does a better job than any of our previous metrics in taking contextual factors into account. The model adjusts for how the park affects performance, but also for things like the talent of the opposing pitcher, value of different types of batted-ball events, league, temperature and other factors. It's able to describe a player's expected offensive contribution than any other statistic we've found over the years, and also does a better job of predicting future performance as well.

The other aspect of run-scoring is baserunning, which we quantify using Baserunning Runs. BRR not only records the value of stolen bases (or getting caught in the act), but also accounts for all the stuff that doesn't show up on the back of a baseball card: a runner's ability to go first to third on a single, or advance on a fly ball.

Defense

Where offensive value is *relatively* easy to identify and understand, defensive value is … not. Over the past dozen years, the sabermetric community has focused mostly on stats based on zone data: a real-live human person records the type of batted ball and estimated landing location, and models are created that give expected outs. From there, you can compare fielders' actual outs to those expected ones. Simple, right?

Unfortunately, zone data has two major issues. First, zone data is recorded by commercial data providers who keep the raw data private unless you pay for it. (All the statistics we build in this book and on our website use public data as inputs.) That hurts our ability to test assumptions or duplicate results. Second, over the years it has become apparent that there's quite a bit of "noise" in zone-based fielding analysis. Sometimes the conclusions drawn from zone data don't hold up to scrutiny, and sometimes the different data provided by different providers don't look anything alike, giving wildly different results. Sometimes the hard-working professional stringers or scorers might unknowingly inflict unconscious bias into the mix: for example good fielders will often be credited with more expected outs despite the data, and ballparks with high press boxes tend to score more line drives than ones with a lower press box.

Enter our Fielding Runs Above Average (FRAA). For most positions, FRAA is built from play-by-play data, which allows us to avoid the subjectivity found in many other fielding metrics. The idea is this: count how many fielding plays are made by a given player and compare that to expected plays for an average fielder at their position (based on pitcher ground ball tendencies and batter handedness). Then we adjust for park and base-out situations.

When it comes to catchers, our methodology is a little different thanks to the laundry list of responsibilities they're tasked with beyond just, well, catching and throwing the ball. By now you've probably heard about "framing" or the art of making umpires more likely to call balls outside the strike zone for strikes. To put this into one tidy number, we incorporate pitch tracking data (for the years it exists) and adjust for important factors like pitcher, umpire, batter and home-field advantage using a mixed-model approach. This grants us a number for how many strikes the catcher is personally adding to (or subtracting from) his pitchers' performance … which we then convert to runs added or lost using linear weights.

Framing is one of the biggest parts of determining catcher value, but we also take into account blocking balls from going past, whether a scorer deems it a passed ball or a wild pitch. We use a similar approach—one that really benefits from the pitch tracking data that tells us what ends up in the dirt and what doesn't. We also include a catcher's ability to prevent stolen bases and how well they field balls in play, and *finally* we come up with our FRAA for catchers.

Pitching

Both pitching and fielding make up the half of baseball that isn't run scoring: run prevention. Separating pitching from fielding is a tough task, and most recent pitching analysis has branched off from Voros McCracken's famous (and controversial) statement, "There is little if any difference among major-league pitchers in their ability to prevent hits on balls hit in the field of play." The research of the analytic community has validated this to some extent, and there are a host of "defense-independent" pitching measures that have been developed to try and extract the effect of the defense behind a hurler from the pitcher's work.

Our solution to this quandary is Deserved Run Average (DRA), our core pitching metric. DRA seeks to evaluate a pitcher's performance, much like earned run average (ERA), the tried-and-true pitching stat you've seen on every baseball broadcast or box score from the past century, but it's very different. To start, DRA takes an event-by-event look at what the pitchers does, and adjusts the value of that event based on different environmental factors like park, batter, catcher, umpire, base-out situation, run differential, inning, defense, home field advantage, pitcher role and temperature. That mixed model gives us a pitcher's expected contribution, similar to what we do for our DRC+ model for hitters and FRAA model for catchers. (Oh, and we also consider the pitcher's effect on basestealing and on balls getting past the catcher.)

DRA is set to the scale of runs allowed per nine innings (RA9) instead of ERA, which makes DRA's scale slightly higher than ERA's. Because of this, for ease of use, we're supplying DRA-, which is much easier for the reader to parse. As with DRC+, DRA- is an "index" stat, meaning instead of using some arbitrary and shifting number to denote what's "good," average is always 100. The reason that it uses a minus rather than a plus is because like ERA, a lower number is better. Therefore a 75 DRA- describes a performance 25 percent better than average, whereas a 150 DRA- means that either a pitcher is getting extremely lucky with their results, or getting ready to try a new pitch.

Since the last time you picked up an edition of this book, we've also made a few minor changes to DRA to make it better. Recent research into "tunneling"—the act of throwing consecutive pitches that appear similar from a batter's point of view until after the swing decision point–data has given us a new contextual factor to account for in DRA: plate distance. This refers to the distance between successive pitches as they approach the plate, and while it has a smaller effect than factors like velocity or whiff rate, it still can help explain pitcher strikeout rate in our model.

Recently Added Descriptive Statistics

Returning to our 2021 edition of the book are a few figures which recently appeared. These numbers may be a little bit more familiar to those of you who have spent some time investigating baseball statistics.

Fastball Percentage

Our fastball percentage (FA%) statistic measures how frequently a pitcher throws a pitch classified as a "fastball," measured as a percentage of overall pitches thrown. We qualify three types of fastballs:

1. The traditional four-seam fastball;
2. The two-seam fastball or sinker;
3. "Hard cutters," which are pitches that have the movement profile of a cut fastball and are used as the pitcher's primary offering or in place of a more traditional fastball.

For example, a pitcher with a FA% of 67 throws any combination of these three pitches about two-thirds of the time.

Whiff Rate

Everybody loves a swing and a miss, and whiff rate (Whiff%) measures how frequently pitchers induce a swinging strike. To calculate Whiff%, we add up all the pitches thrown that ended with a swinging strike, then divide that number by a pitcher's total pitches thrown. Most often, high whiff rates correlate with high strikeout rates (and overall effective pitcher performance).

Called Strike Probability

Called Strike Probability (CSP) is a number that represents the likelihood that all of a pitcher's pitches will be called a strike while controlling for location, pitcher and batter handedness, umpire and count. Here's how it works: on each pitch, our model determines how many times (out of 100) that a similar pitch was called for a strike given those factors mentioned above, and when normalized for each batter's strike zone. Then we average the CSP for all pitches thrown by a pitcher in a season, and that gives us the yearly CSP percentage you see in the stats boxes.

As you might imagine, pitchers with a higher CSP are more likely to work in the zone, where pitchers with a lower CSP are likely locating their pitches outside the normal strike zone, for better or for worse.

Projections

Many of you aren't turning to this book just for a look at what a player has done, but for a look at what a player is going to do: the PECOTA projections. PECOTA, initially developed by Nate Silver (who has moved on to greater fame as a political analyst), consists of three parts:

1. Major-league equivalencies, which use minor-league statistics to project how a player will perform in the major leagues;
2. Baseline forecasts, which use weighted averages and regression to the mean to estimate a player's current true talent level; and
3. Aging curves, which uses the career paths of comparable players to estimate how a player's statistics are likely to change over time.

With all those important things covered, let's take a look at what's in the book this year.

Team Prospectus

Most of this book is composed of team chapters, with one for each of the 30 major-league franchises. On the first page of each chapter, you'll see a box that contains some of the key statistics for each team as well as a very inviting stadium diagram.

We start with the team name, their unadjusted 2020 win-loss record, and their divisional ranking. Beneath that are a host of other team statistics. **Pythag** presents an adjusted 2020 winning percentage, calculated by taking runs scored per game (**RS/G**) and runs allowed per game (**RA/G**) for the team, and running them through a version of Bill James' Pythagorean formula that was refined and improved by David Smyth and Brandon Heipp. (The formula is called "Pythagenpat," which is equally fun to type and to say.)

Next up is **DRC+**, described earlier, to indicate the overall hitting ability of the team either above or below league-average. Run prevention on the pitching side is covered by **DRA** (also mentioned earlier) and another metric: Fielding Independent Pitching (**FIP**), which calculates another ERA-like statistic based on strikeouts, walks, and home runs recorded. Defensive Efficiency Rating (**DER**) tells us the percentage of balls in play turned into outs for the team, and is a quick fielding shorthand that rounds out run prevention.

After that, we have several measures related to roster composition, as opposed to on-field performance. **B-Age** and **P-Age** tell us the average age of a team's batters and pitchers, respectively. **Payroll** is the combined team payroll for all on-field players, and Doug Pappas' Marginal Dollars per Marginal Win (**M$/MW**) tells us how much money a team spent to earn production above replacement level.

Next to each of these stats, we've listed each team's MLB rank in that category from first to 30th. In this, first always indicates a positive outcome and 30th a negative outcome, except in the case of salary—first is highest.

After the franchise statistics, we share a few items about the team's home ballpark. There's the aforementioned diagram of the park's dimensions (including distances to the outfield wall), a graphic showing the height of the wall from the left-field pole to the right-field pole, and a table showing three-year park factors for the stadium. The park factors are displayed as indexes where 100 is average, 110 means that the park inflates the statistic in question by 10 percent, and 90 means that the park deflates the statistic in question by 10 percent.

On the second page of each team chapter, you'll find three graphs. The first is **Payroll History** and helps you see how the team's payroll has compared to the MLB and divisional average payrolls over time. Payroll figures are current as of January 1, 2021; with so many free agents still unsigned as of this writing, the final 2021 figure will likely be significantly different for many teams. (In the meantime, you can always find the most current data at Baseball Prospectus' Cot's Baseball Contracts page.)

The second graph is **Future Commitments** and helps you see the team's future outlays, if any.

The third graph is **Farm System Ranking** and displays how the Baseball Prospectus prospect team has ranked the organization's farm system since 2007.

After the graphs, we have a **Personnel** section that lists many of the important decision-makers and upper-level field and operations staff members for the franchise, as well as any former Baseball Prospectus staff members who are currently part of the organization. (In very rare circumstances, someone might be on both lists!)

Position Players

After all that information and a thoughtful bylined essay covering each team, we present our player comments. These are also bylined, but due to frequent franchise shifts during the offseason, our bylines are more a rough guide than a perfect accounting of who wrote what.

Each player is listed with the major-league team that employed him as of early January 2021. If a player changed teams after that point via free agency, trade, or any other method, you'll be able to find them in the chapter for their previous squad.

As an example, take a look at the player comment for Padres shortstop Fernando Tatis Jr.: the stat block that accompanies his written comment is at the top of this page. First we cover biographical information (age is as of June 30, 2021) before moving onto the stats themselves. Our statistic columns include standard identifying information like **YEAR**, **TEAM**, **LVL** (level of affiliated play) and **AGE** before getting into the numbers. Next, we provide raw, untranslated

Fernando Tatis Jr. SS

Born: 01/02/99 Age: 22 Bats: R Throws: R
Height: 6'3" Weight: 217 Origin: International Free Agent, 2015

YEAR	TEAM	LVL	AGE	PA	R	2B	3B	HR	RBI	BB	K	SB	CS	AVG/OBP/SLG
2018	SA	AA	19	394	77	22	4	16	43	33	109	16	5	.286/.355/.507
2019	SD	MLB	20	372	61	13	6	22	53	30	110	16	6	.317/.379/.590
2020	SD	MLB	21	257	50	11	2	17	45	27	61	11	3	.277/.366/.571
2021 FS	SD	MLB	22	600	95	24	4	31	81	50	165	17	8	.263/.331/.499
2021 DC	SD	MLB	22	628	100	25	4	32	85	53	173	19	8	.263/.331/.499

Comparables: Darryl Strawberry, Bo Bichette, Ronald Acuña Jr.

YEAR	TEAM	LVL	AGE	PA	DRC+	BABIP	BRR	FRAA	WARP
2018	SA	AA	19	394	136	.370	3.0	SS(83): -1.9	2.4
2019	SD	MLB	20	372	118	.410	7.1	SS(83): 0.9	3.4
2020	SD	MLB	21	257	126	.306	0.7	SS(57): -5.5	0.9
2021 FS	SD	MLB	22	600	126	.318	1.7	SS -1	3.9
2021 DC	SD	MLB	22	628	126	.318	1.8	SS -1	4.0

numbers like you might find on the back of your dad's baseball cards: **PA** (plate appearances), **R** (runs), **2B** (doubles), **3B** (triples), **HR** (home runs), **RBI** (runs batted in), **BB** (walks), **K** (strikeouts), **SB** (stolen bases) and **CS** (caught stealing).

Following the basic stats is **Whiff%** (whiff rate), which denotes how often, when a batter swings, he fails to make contact with the ball. Another way to think of this number is an inverse of a hitter's contact rate.

Next, we have unadjusted "slash" statistics: **AVG** (batting average), **OBP** (on-base percentage) and **SLG** (slugging percentage). Following the slash line is **DRC+** (Deserved Runs Created Plus), which we described earlier as total offensive expected contribution compared to the league average.

BABIP (batting average on balls in play) tells us how often a ball in play fell for a hit, and can help us identify whether a batter may have been lucky or not ... but note that high BABIPs also tend to follow the great hitters of our time, as well as speedy singles hitters who put the ball on the ground.

The next item is **BRR** (Baserunning Runs), which covers all of a player's baserunning accomplishments including (but not limited to) swiped bags and failed attempts. Next is **FRAA** (Fielding Runs Above Average), which also includes the number of games previously played at each position noted in parentheses. Multi-position players have only their two most frequent positions listed here, but their total FRAA number reflects all positions played.

Our last column here is **WARP** (Wins Above Replacement Player). WARP estimates the total value of a player, which means for hitters it takes into account hitting runs above average (calculated using the DRC+ model), BRR and FRAA. Then, it makes an adjustment for positions played and gives the player a credit for plate appearances based upon the difference between "replacement level"—which is derived from the quality of players added to a team's roster after the start of the season–and the league average.

The final line just below the stats box is **PECOTA** data, which is discussed further in a following section.

Catchers

Catchers are a special breed, and thus they have earned their own separate box which displays some of the defensive metrics that we've built just for them. As an example, let's check out Yasmani Grandal.

YEAR	TEAM	P. COUNT	FRM RUNS	BLK RUNS	THRW RUNS	TOT RUNS
2018	LAD	16816	15.7	0.8	0.1	16.5
2019	MIL	18740	19.4	1.8	-0.1	21.1
2020	CHW	4830	3.7	0.3	-0.2	3.8
2021	CHW	14430	16.7	-0.6	1.0	17.1
2021	CHW	14430	16.7	0.4	1.0	18.0

The **YEAR** and **TEAM** columns match what you'd find in the other stat box. **P. COUNT** indicates the number of pitches thrown while the catcher was behind the plate, including swinging strikes, fouls and balls in play. **FRM RUNS** is the total run value the catcher provided (or cost) his team by influencing the umpire to call strikes where other catchers did not. **BLK RUNS** expresses the total run value above or below average for the catcher's ability to prevent wild pitches and passed balls. **THRW RUNS** is calculated using a similar model as the previous two statistics, and it measures a catcher's ability to throw out basestealers but also to dissuade them from testing his arm in the first place. It takes into account factors like the pitcher (including his delivery and pickoff move) and baserunner (who could be as fast as Billy Hamilton or as slow as Yonder Alonso). **TOT RUNS** is the sum of all of the previous three statistics.

Pitchers

Let's give our pitchers a turn, using 2020 AL Cy Young winner Shane Bieber as our example. Take a look at his stat block: the first line and the **YEAR**, **TEAM**, **LVL** and **AGE** columns are the same as in the position player example earlier.

Here too, we have a series of columns that display raw, unadjusted statistics compiled by the pitcher over the course of a season: **W** (wins), **L** (losses), **SV** (saves), **G** (games pitched), **GS** (games started), **IP** (innings pitched), **H** (hits allowed) and **HR** (home runs allowed). Next we have two statistics that are rates: **BB/9** (walks per nine innings) and **K/9** (strikeouts per nine innings), before returning to the unadjusted K (strikeouts).

Next up is **GB%** (ground ball percentage), which is the percentage of all batted balls that were hit on the ground, including both outs and hits. Remember, this is based on observational data and subject to human error, so please approach this with a healthy dose of skepticism.

BABIP (batting average on balls in play) is calculated using the same methodology as it is for position players, but it often tells us more about a pitcher than it does a hitter. With pitchers, a high BABIP is often due to poor defense or bad luck, and can often be an indicator of potential rebound, and a low BABIP may be cause to expect performance regression. (A typical league-average BABIP is close to .290-.300.)

The metrics **WHIP** (walks plus hits per inning pitched) and **ERA** (earned run average) are old standbys: WHIP measures walks and hits allowed on a per-inning basis, while ERA measures earned runs on a nine-inning basis. Neither of these stats are translated or adjusted.

DRA- (Deserved Run Average) was described at length earlier, and measures how the pitcher "deserved" to perform compared to other pitchers. Please note that since we lack all the data points that would make for a "real" DRA for minor-league events, the DRA- displayed for minor league partial-seasons is based off of different data. (That data is a modified version of our cFIP metric, which you can find more information about on our website.)

Shane Bieber   RHP

Born: 05/31/95   Age: 26   Bats: R   Throws: R
Height: 6'3"   Weight: 200   Origin: Round 4, 2016 Draft (#122 overall)

YEAR	TEAM	LVL	AGE	W	L	SV	G	GS	IP	H	HR	BB/9	K/9	K	GB%	BABIP
2018	AKR	AA	23	3	0	0	5	5	31	26	1	0.3	8.7	30	47.3%	.278
2018	COL	AAA	23	3	1	0	8	8	48[2]	30	3	1.1	8.7	47	52.0%	.227
2018	CLE	MLB	23	11	5	0	20	19	114[2]	130	13	1.8	9.3	118	46.2%	.356
2019	CLE	MLB	24	15	8	0	34	33	214[1]	186	31	1.7	10.9	259	44.4%	.298
2020	CLE	MLB	25	8	1	0	12	12	77[1]	46	7	2.4	14.2	122	48.4%	.267
2021 FS	CLE	MLB	26	10	6	0	26	26	150	121	18	2.1	11.7	195	45.5%	.297
2021 DC	CLE	MLB	26	14	7	0	30	30	196.7	159	24	2.1	11.7	257	45.5%	.297

Comparables: Luis Severino, Danny Salazar, Joe Musgrove

YEAR	TEAM	LVL	AGE	WHIP	ERA	DRA-	WARP	MPH	FB%	WHF	CSP
2018	AKR	AA	23	0.87	1.16	61	0.9				
2018	COL	AAA	23	0.74	1.66	69	1.2				
2018	CLE	MLB	23	1.33	4.55	74	2.6	94.7	57.4%	26.2%	
2019	CLE	MLB	24	1.05	3.28	75	4.9	94.4	45.8%	30.8%	
2020	CLE	MLB	25	0.87	1.63	53	2.6	95.3	53.6%	40.7%	
2021 FS	CLE	MLB	26	1.04	2.44	64	4.4	94.7	50.0%	33.2%	44.2%
2021 DC	CLE	MLB	26	1.04	2.44	64	5.8	94.7	50.0%	33.2%	44.2%

Just like with hitters, **WARP** (Wins Above Replacement Player) is a total value metric that puts pitchers of all stripes on the same scale as position players. We use DRA as the primary input for our calculation of WARP. You might notice that relief pitchers (due to their limited innings) may have a lower WARP than you were expecting or than you might see in other WARP-like metrics. WARP does not take leverage into account, just the actions a pitcher performs and the expected value of those actions ... which ends up judging high-leverage relief pitchers differently than you might imagine given their prestige and market value.

MPH gives you the pitcher's 95th percentile velocity for the noted season, in order to give you an idea of what the *peak* fastball velocity a pitcher possesses. Since this comes from our pitch-tracking data, it is not publicly available for minor-league pitchers.

Finally, we display the three new pitching metrics we described earlier. **FB%** (fastball percentage) gives you the percentage of fastballs thrown out of all pitches. **WHF** (whiff rate) tells you the percentage of swinging strikes induced out of all pitches. **CSP** (called strike probability) expresses the likelihood of all pitches thrown to result in a called strike, after controlling for factors like handedness, umpire, pitch type, count and location.

PECOTA

All players have PECOTA projections for 2021, as well as a set of other numbers that describe the performance of comparable players according to PECOTA. All projections for 2021 are for the player at the date we went to press in early January and are projected into the league and park context as indicated by the team abbreviation. (Note that players at very low levels of the minors are too unpredictable to assess using these numbers.) All PECOTA projected statistics represent a player's projected major-league performance.

How we're doing that is a little different this season. There are really two different values that go into the final stat line that you see for PECOTA: How a player performs, and how much playing time he'll be given to perform it. In the past we've estimated playing time based on each team's roster and depth charts, and we'll continue to do that. These projections are denoted as **2021 DC**.

But in many cases, a player won't be projected for major-league playing time; most of the time this is because they aren't projected to be major-league players at all, but still developing as prospects. Or perhaps a player will provide Triple-A depth, only to have an opportunity open up because of injury. For these purposes, we're also supplying a second projection, labeled **2021 FS**, or full season. This is what we would project the player to provide in 600 plate appearances or 150 innings pitched.

Below the projections are the player's three highest-scoring comparable players as determined by PECOTA. All comparables represent a snapshot of how the listed player was performing at the same age as the current player, so if a

23-year-old pitcher is compared to Bartolo Colón, he's actually being compared to a 23-year-old Colón, not the version that pitched for the Rangers in 2018, nor to Colón's career as a whole.

A few points about pitcher projections. First, we aren't yet projecting peak velocity, so that column will be blank in the PECOTA lines. Second, projecting DRA is trickier than evaluating past performance, because it is unclear how deserving each pitcher will be of his anticipated outcomes. However, we know that another DRA-related statistic–contextual FIP or cFIP–estimates future run scoring very well. So for PECOTA, the projected DRA- figures you see are based on the past cFIPs generated by the pitcher and comparable players over time, along with the other factors described above.

If you're familiar with PECOTA, then you'll have noticed that the projection system often appears bullish on players coming off a bad year and bearish on players coming off a good year. (This is because the system weights several previous seasons, not just the most recent one.) In addition, we publish the 50th percentile projections for each player–which is smack in the middle of the range of projected production—which tends to mean PECOTA stat lines don't often have extreme results like 40 home runs or 250 strikeouts in a given season. In essence, PECOTA doesn't project very many extreme seasons.

Managers

After all those wonderful team chapters, we've got statistics for each big-league manager, all of whom are organized by alphabetical order. Here you'll find a block including an extraordinary amount of information collected from each manager's entire career. For more information on the acronyms and what they mean, please visit the Glossary at www.baseballprospectus.com.

There is one important metric that we'd like to call attention to, and you'll find it next to each manager's name: **wRM+** (weighted reliever management plus). Developed by Rob Arthur and Rian Watt, wRM+ investigates how good a manager is at using their best relievers during the moments of highest leverage, using both our proprietary DRA metric as well as Leverage Index. wRM+ is scaled to a league average of 100, and a wRM+ of 105 indicates that relievers were used approximately five percent "better" than average. On the other hand, a wRM+ of 95 would tell us the team used its relievers five percent "worse" than the average team.

While wRM+ does not have an extremely strong correlation with a manager, it is statistically significant; this means that a manager is not *entirely* responsible for a team's wRM+, but does have some effect on that number.

Part 1: Team Analysis

Performance Graphs

Payroll History (in millions)

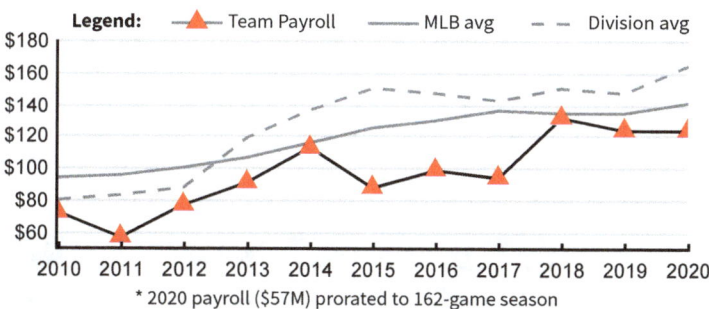

* 2020 payroll ($57M) prorated to 162-game season

Future Commitments (in millions)

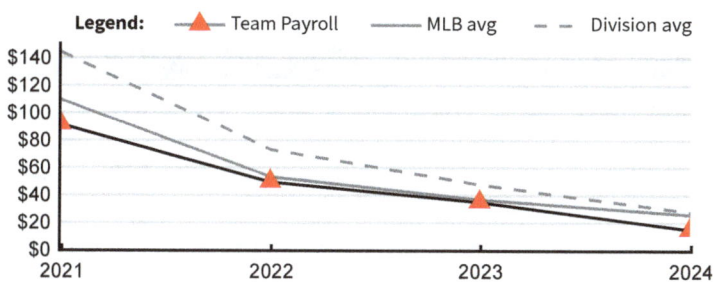

Farm System Ranking

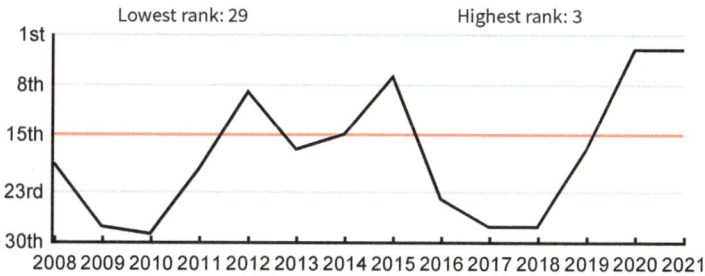

2020 Team Performance

ACTUAL STANDINGS

Team	W	L	Pct
LAD	43	17	0.717
SD	37	23	0.617
SF	29	31	0.483
COL	26	34	0.433
ARI	**25**	**35**	**0.417**

dWIN% STANDINGS

Team	W	L	Pct
LAD	37	23	0.624
SD	34	26	0.567
SF	27	33	0.465
ARI	**23**	**37**	**0.386**
COL	22	38	0.375

TOP HITTERS

Player	WARP
Kole Calhoun	1.6
Christian Walker	0.9
Ketel Marte	0.8

TOP PITCHERS

Player	WARP
Zac Gallen	1.5
Merrill Kelly	0.5
Stefan Crichton	0.4

VITAL STATISTICS

Statistic Name	Value	Rank
Pythagenpat	.456	23rd
dWin%	.386	25th
Runs Scored per Game	4.48	19th
Runs Allowed per Game	4.92	17th
Deserved Runs Created Plus	95	20th
Deserved Run Average Minus	111	26th
Fielding Independent Pitching	4.99	23rd
Defensive Efficiency Rating	.697	19th
Batter Age	29.7	27th
Pitcher Age	28.0	18th
Payroll	$57.0M	15th
Marginal $ per Marginal Win	$5.6M	23rd

2021 Team Projections

PROJECTED STANDINGS

Team	W	L	Pct	+/-
LAD	104.4	57.6	0.644	-11
With Dustin May ready and David Price returning, adding Trevor Bauer was purely lapidary. Still, they're almost alone in their willingness to put up or shut up.				
SD	95.4	66.6	0.589	-4
Not just Blake Snell, but Yu Darvish and Joe Musgrove; not just Ha-Seong Kim, but Jurickson Profar, all without trading a starting player.				
ARI	**79.2**	**82.8**	**0.489**	**11**
Mike Hazen is a good trader, but ownership continues to confine him to corner-store bartering.				
SF	74.9	87.1	0.462	-3
Most of their individual moves were small, but the Giants' winter work amounts to the first step toward pivoting from a rebuild to contending.				
COL	58.9	103.1	0.364	-11
The time was ripe for a rebuild, but the return for Nolan Arenado is not a confidence-inspiring start.				

TOP PROJECTED HITTERS

Player	WARP
Ketel Marte	3.3
Daulton Varsho	2.5
Kole Calhoun	2.0

TOP PROJECTED PITCHERS

Player	WARP
Zac Gallen	3.2
Luke Weaver	1.7
Madison Bumgarner	1.2

FARM SYSTEM REPORT

Top Prospect	Number of Top 101 Prospects
Kristian Robinson, #15	4

KEY DEDUCTIONS

Player	WARP

KEY ADDITIONS

Player	WARP
Joakim Soria	0.8

Team Personnel

President & Chief Executive Officer
Derrick Hall

Executive Vice President & General Manager
Mike Hazen

Sr. Vice President & Assistant General Manager
Amiel Sawdaye

Vice President, Research & Development
Mike Fitzgerald

Manager
Torey Lovullo

BP Alumni
Hudson Belinsky
Tucker Blair
Jason Parks

Chase Field Stats

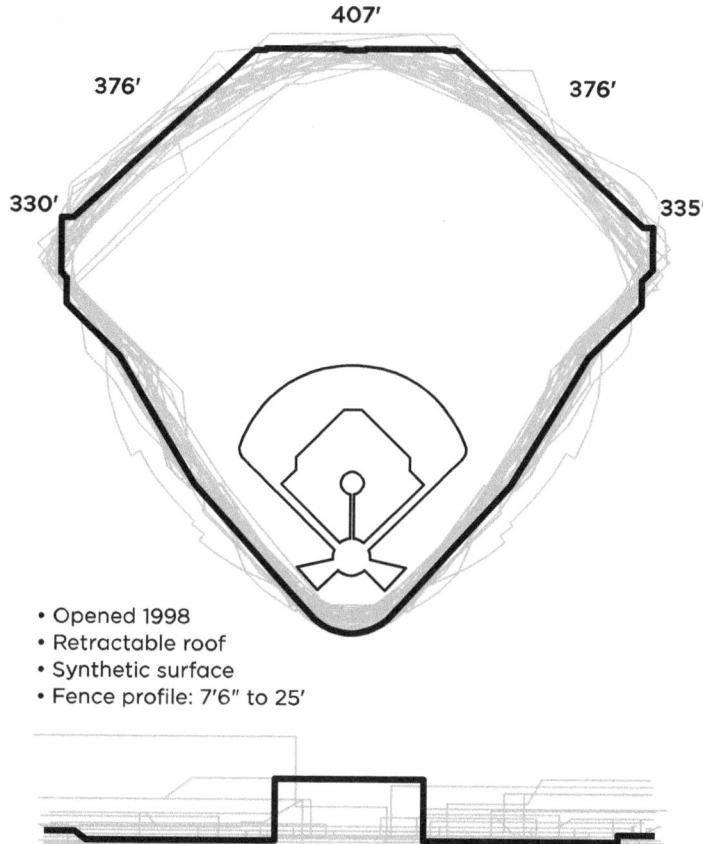

- Opened 1998
- Retractable roof
- Synthetic surface
- Fence profile: 7'6" to 25'

Three-Year Park Factors

Runs	Runs/RH	Runs/LH	HR/RH	HR/LH
103	102	107	100	101

Diamondbacks Team Analysis

The name of the game show is "Hiccup … or the New Normal?", or at least that's what it reads on the two-foot-high neon letters behind you. You're standing behind a podium, not sure how you got there. The lighting is calibrated wrong and oriented directly into your eyeballs. As you grimace and shield your eyes, you look around and realize that you're being watched. The host, the contestants next to you, the studio audience … they're all staring at you, half-annoyed, half-amused and expecting you to say something.

"The Arizona Diamondbacks…", the host says, trying to prompt you. You stare back, trying to reconstruct the last few hours.

You have regrets about eating the packet of powdered gravy you found in the parking lot.

"The Arizona…" he says again, this time followed by a pause, as if it's the very idea of the state of Arizona that's confusing you, which is understandable.

"…Diamondbacks," he finishes.

Oh. You get it. You're supposed to answer the question. Hiccup? Or the new normal? The studio audience shouts along with the second sentence when the host says it. It's a nice touch.

On August 18th, the Arizona Diamondbacks beat the Oakland Athletics, 10-1. They stood two games over .500, with a 13-11 record, firmly in postseason position. It's where most observers expected them to be all along. They were contenders.

On September 9th, they lost to the Dodgers in extra innings. They were 15-29. You don't have to be a mathemagician to realize exactly how horribly they had screwed up over those 22 days. They had won two games and lost a billionty. Even by the standards of 2020, those must have been three looooooooooooooooooooong weeks.

Hiccup? Or the new normal? The applause sign lights up. The studio audience goes wild.

Start with the basic concept that we all understand: You get to ignore 2020 entirely, in every facet of life, in every context, for the rest of eternity. It never existed. If you were born in 2000, you will celebrate your 21st birthday in 2022, and you'll understand completely. Any baby born in the year 2020 will suffer from a *Pirates of Penzance*-like fate because their birth didn't exist in the first place.

But that doesn't mean there weren't enormous, bright, fluttering red flags draped over the Diamondbacks in 2020. The highest on-base percentage from a returning player in next season's lineup was David Peralta's .339, and he had to hit .300 to get there. A dip in a 33-year-old's batting average is all that stands between him feebly leading the team in OBP and being an offensive liability, and he's the best they've got.

The team's misery was compounded by the disastrous season from Madison Bumgarner, who might be one of the team's only significant financial splurges for a while. The front office sized the team up, figured they were a reliable starter short of being a World Series contender, plugged their nose, said a few prayers on behalf of the soft market and took a chance on an over-30 pitcher with a heckuva Wikipedia page and declining velocity. He struck out two batters in his first inning as a Diamondback, and allowed 31 runs in the 40 innings after that. He was the only starter in 2020 with more earned runs than strikeouts, which seems bad.

The lineup was miserable. The pitching acquisitions were dreadful. What's supposed to change?

The new normal. That's your answer. This is the new normal, and it's what the Diamondbacks can expect for the next several years. They bought the wrong pitcher, they have a surprisingly old lineup, an impressive-but-distant farm system and a mid-market payroll chained to their ankle. It's not likely to improve soon.

Except … hold on a second. This was a team that was built by a front office that correctly identified the state of the franchise, one in need of a reload instead of a rebuild. They traded Paul Goldschmidt with a plan, and it looked successful in its first trial run. Christian Walker was an effective, low-budget replacement for the power. Carson Kelly made up for whatever he was lacking. Luke Weaver was going to be a rotation monster for years to come. This was a team that was pointed in the right direction *just a few months ago*. The third-to-last sentence of the Diamondbacks essay in the 2020 Baseball Prospectus Annual was "But if the current indicators are to be trusted at all, it appears that brighter days are ahead."

What changed since then? What reversed the fortunes of the Diamondbacks so drastically? A 60-game season? A three-week stretch that never had time to even out? We've already established that 2020 doesn't count for anything. There were metaphorical mosquitoes the size of basset hounds flying around the entire year, and they sucked us all dry, but they're gone now.

Probably.

Maybe.

This is the still the organization that was confident enough to trade a top-100 prospect like Jazz Chisholm away to get a less-heralded pitcher and have it work out *brilliantly*. Zac Gallen's historic start to his career is proof that the Diamondbacks aren't just smart, they're creative and wily. It takes equal parts moxie and guile to zero in on a pitcher like that, on a rebuilding team that desperately wanted to develop starting pitching, and figure out how to pry him away. That's some nifty sleight of hand.

They correctly scouted Merrill Kelly, local gadfly and KBO veteran, as someone who could get more outs for less money than the typical pitcher, and they committed several million dollars on that belief. It's a move that made them look smart. Let the other teams fight over the expensive starting pitchers like Trevor Bauer and Max Scherzer. The Diamondbacks will find their own pitchers, and they'll be better at it than almost anyone else.

It's a hiccup. Hold your breath, drink a glass of water, eat a spoonful of sugar, stand on your head, do whatever it takes. But this is a hiccup. You open your mouth to announce your answer, and every member of the studio audience leans toward the stage.

But, wait wait wait wait waaaaait a second. Have you noticed how sneaky-old the Diamondbacks' lineup is for a team that's in a reload/rebuild? Kole Calhoun, one of their leading power sources, is 33. Christian Walker will turn 30 by the time the season starts. Peralta turns 34 in August. Eduardo Escobar—one of the most disappointing players in a season filled with disappointment on all sides—will be 32, and it's not like this was his only bad year out of the last 10. He's a relatively recent discovery, only transcending the super-utility label a couple of years ago. The offensive emergence of Nick Ahmed turned him into a ridiculously valuable two-way player, but he'll be 31, and this doesn't have to last forever.

Now look for the next wave. Daulton Varsho might be here to stay, Pavin Smith made his debut and Geraldo Perdomo looks like he could make the 2021 roster at some point. But this is still a young farm system, at least on the offensive side, and a collection that missed out on a year's worth of development in live ball. Kristian Robinson is only 20. Corbin Carroll and Alek Thomas are both under 21, and they've never played in the upper minors. They certainly could constitute the next wave of magical snakes. But they could also be a latter-day Conor Jackson/Carlos Quentin/Stephen Drew, who accumulate a few wins over their careers, but far away from Phoenix. Don't count your prospects before they debut.

It might be two years before the farm system bears fruit. Maybe three. Maybe never.

This is the new normal. The entire franchise is going to sink into a boggy pit, employing all their tricks and talent to keep their head above the surface, and the Dodgers will do a little goat dance around them for the next 30 years or so. They're old and cheap, and they haven't proven that they can spin prospect straw into major-league gold, so there's no reason to assume they can. It wouldn't be surprising, but it isn't something to place a large cash wager on. It never is without evidence.

And when the Dodgers are dancing around them, the already-rich Giants might be reborn. The Padres have already made the transition from perennial laughingstock to powerhouse, apparently, and though they've behaved like a small market in the past, they're now the only professional sports team in a metropolitan area of three million souls. The Rockies might … look, every single mother of everyone involved with the Rockies is very, very proud of everything they've accomplished.

As you start to announce your answer, you realize it's the dumbest thing you've ever heard. A top-third farm system isn't enough to have hope, especially when it's coupled with a new, forward-thinking front office that's already demonstrated a knack for finding hidden or unheralded talent? Poppycock.

The Diamondbacks don't need to ape the Dodgers. They don't need to spend as much as the Giants might in the future. They just need to spit out a bunch of prospects, like the Padres did, to get good. And make the same kind of prudent, creative trades that the new regime has already made. That's it. That's the secret sauce. The reason the Rays were capable of winning a pennant, and why the A's were contenders to do the same, is that baseball is still set up to screw young players. The under-30 players are usually the best players, and they're paid the least, by design. Get the good players, keep them for a few years while watering the good-player plants in the garden, then trade the good players for more good-player plants. It's not a novel idea, but it sure does work.

If the Diamondbacks are really run by smart people, from the front office to the coaching staff, they'll elbow their way into the conversation, just like they've done in the past. This is the franchise that lost 97 games in their first season and won 100 games in the next. They lost 97 games in 2010 and won the division in 2011. They lost 93 games in 2016, then won 93 games in 2017.

Why, they keep rising from the ashes like some sort of … mythical … ash-rising creature. If you believe in the front office, you believe in their ability to be better than expected, sooner than expected. The question isn't "Hiccup … or the New Normal?" It's *do you believe in this front office's ability to find and secure baseball talent*? They have a surprisingly impressive resume so far. And if you believe in that ability, then, yeah, it's a hiccup.

Just know that the margin of error for the Arizona Diamondbacks is freakishly thin. They're chasing the richest, smartest, most successful team in the land. They're pitted against the Giants, another financial powerhouse with a front office that sprung from the Dodgers' thigh, like Dionysus from Zeus. They have to overcome another franchise, the Padres, that has to do the same prospect-to-production trick that the Diamondbacks have to pull off, except they've already done it. And they also have to match up against the Rockies, who play in a city that "was named the best place to live in the United States by U.S. News & World Report[22]," according to Wikipedia.

You refuse to answer the question. There are no hiccups. There is no new normal. There is only baseball, and the Diamondbacks might have an idea of how to play baseball better than other teams. Just give them time.

The host scowls at your announcement. No one has ever refused to answer the question before. But he shakes it off and turns over the next index card, after docking you 20 points.

The year … 2020? Hiccup? Or the new normal?

You look at the studio audience. Everyone is smiling, but they're gross, malevolent smiles, with arched eyebrows and sunken eyes. They flash mouths filled with sharp teeth, as if they'd all been filed into a point.

The host turns to you expectantly after the other contestant said something that you didn't hear. Now it's your turn. Hiccup? Or the new normal? Your brain sinks into your stomach. You'd like to go home now.

—*Grant Brisbee writes about the San Francisco Giants for The Athletic.*

Part 2: Player Analysis

Arizona Diamondbacks 2021

PLAYER COMMENTS WITH GRAPHS

Nick Ahmed SS
Born: 03/15/90   Age: 31   Bats: R   Throws: R
Height: 6'2"   Weight: 200   Origin: Round 2, 2011 Draft (#85 overall)

YEAR	TEAM	LVL	AGE	PA	R	2B	3B	HR	RBI	BB	K	SB	CS	AVG/OBP/SLG
2018	ARI	MLB	28	564	61	33	5	16	70	40	109	5	4	.234/.290/.411
2019	ARI	MLB	29	625	79	33	6	19	82	52	113	8	2	.254/.316/.437
2020	ARI	MLB	30	217	29	10	1	5	29	18	46	4	0	.266/.327/.402
2021 FS	ARI	MLB	31	600	66	25	3	15	68	45	132	8	4	.233/.295/.377
2021 DC	ARI	MLB	31	541	60	22	3	14	61	41	119	7	4	.233/.295/.377

Comparables: Royce Clayton, Greg Gagne, Angel Berroa

 The Diamondbacks have had a lot of choices present themselves at shortstop over the years. Would they go with Chris Owings or Didi Gregorius? They chose Owings who then slid quickly to second to make more permanent space for Ahmed. Faced with another future fork in the road, the team wasted no time in moving first-overall pick Dansby Swanson. Arizona even dealt the rising Jazz Chisholm before he could face off with Ahmed for duties at the six. It can seem as if Ahmed has been the incumbent about as often as Dianne Feinstein and, after signing an extension in the offseason, should retain his seat for the foreseeable future. Will Geraldo Perdomo eventually take the torch? History, at the very least, remains on Ahmed's side.

YEAR	TEAM	LVL	AGE	PA	DRC+	BABIP	BRR	FRAA	WARP
2018	ARI	MLB	28	564	89	.265	-0.4	SS(148): 15.1	3.3
2019	ARI	MLB	29	625	92	.280	2.4	SS(158): 6.0	3.2
2020	ARI	MLB	30	217	85	.324	0.3	SS(57): -6.1	-0.5
2021 FS	ARI	MLB	31	600	85	.278	0.4	SS 2	0.9
2021 DC	ARI	MLB	31	541	85	.278	0.4	SS 2	0.8

Nick Ahmed, continued

Batted Ball Distribution

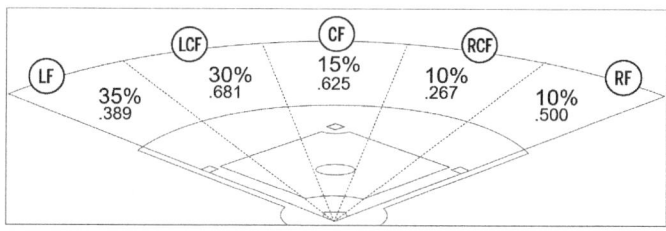

Strike Zone vs LHP   Strike Zone vs RHP

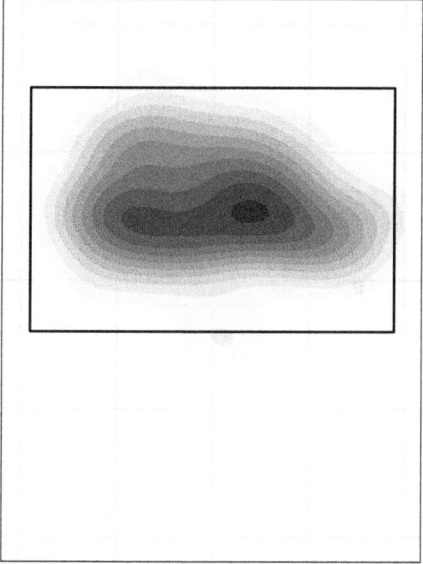

Arizona Diamondbacks 2021

Kole Calhoun RF
Born: 10/14/87 Age: 33 Bats: L Throws: L
Height: 5'10" Weight: 210 Origin: Round 8, 2010 Draft (#264 overall)

YEAR	TEAM	LVL	AGE	PA	R	2B	3B	HR	RBI	BB	K	SB	CS	AVG/OBP/SLG
2018	LAA	MLB	30	552	71	18	2	19	57	53	133	6	2	.208/.283/.369
2019	LAA	MLB	31	632	92	29	1	33	74	70	162	4	1	.232/.325/.467
2020	ARI	MLB	32	228	35	9	0	16	40	28	50	1	1	.226/.338/.526
2021 FS	ARI	MLB	33	600	83	25	4	24	78	62	147	4	2	.237/.327/.441
2021 DC	ARI	MLB	33	597	83	25	4	24	78	62	146	4	2	.237/.327/.441

Comparables: Michael Cuddyer, Jeffrey Hammonds, Cody Ross

Human civilization has been strolling the face of the earth for quite a long time. The strolling takes place simply because we're all quite literally stuck to earth's crust. We don't float, we can't fly, and most of us get a rude reminder of this when we recognize we don't jump as high as we once did. But until the 17th century no one entirely knew why. It was Newton's work, of course, that settled it all. He determined that gravity was a real thing and that what went up must certainly come down. Calhoun was happy in 2020 to showcase that the inverse can also be true as he soared to unfamiliar heights in his first season in the desert, posting career highs in DRC+ (127), slugging percentage (.526), and walk rate (12.3 percent)

YEAR	TEAM	LVL	AGE	PA	DRC+	BABIP	BRR	FRAA	WARP
2018	LAA	MLB	30	552	85	.241	-0.2	RF(136): -3.7, CF(4): -0.2	-0.2
2019	LAA	MLB	31	632	110	.265	0.6	RF(150): 7.2, CF(2): -0.1	3.1
2020	ARI	MLB	32	228	126	.211	0.1	RF(48): 2.9	1.6
2021 FS	ARI	MLB	33	600	109	.283	0.0	RF 1, CF 0	2.1
2021 DC	ARI	MLB	33	597	109	.283	0.0	RF 1	2.0

Kole Calhoun, continued

Batted Ball Distribution

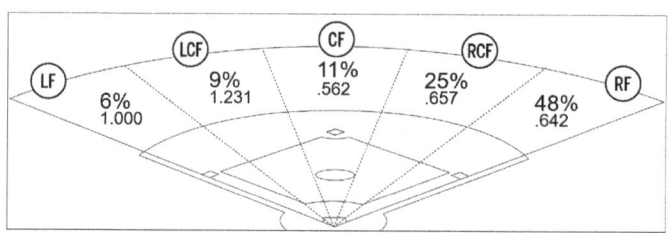

Strike Zone vs LHP   Strike Zone vs RHP

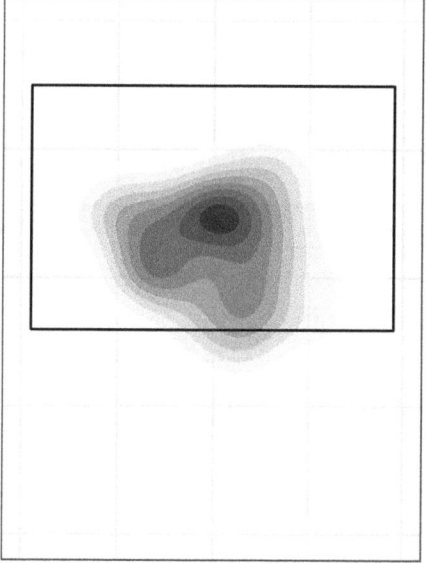

Eduardo Escobar 3B

Born: 01/05/89   Age: 32   Bats: S   Throws: R
Height: 5'10"   Weight: 210   Origin: International Free Agent, 2006

YEAR	TEAM	LVL	AGE	PA	R	2B	3B	HR	RBI	BB	K	SB	CS	AVG/OBP/SLG
2018	MIN	MLB	29	408	45	37	3	15	63	34	91	1	3	.274/.338/.514
2018	ARI	MLB	29	223	30	11	0	8	21	18	35	1	1	.268/.327/.444
2019	ARI	MLB	30	699	94	29	10	35	118	50	130	5	1	.269/.320/.511
2020	ARI	MLB	31	222	22	7	3	4	20	15	41	1	0	.212/.270/.335
2021 FS	ARI	MLB	32	600	70	24	5	19	76	43	127	4	2	.241/.300/.411
2021 DC	ARI	MLB	32	543	63	22	4	17	69	39	115	4	2	.241/.300/.411

Comparables: Greg Dobbs, Larry Parrish, Max Alvis

A 60-game season is tough. We are so used to drawing conclusions on a bigger sample that having confidence in such a tightly framed snapshot is difficult. Then there are guys like Escobar where, after watching him play, you thought to yourself, "Thank goodness it's over," when the season came to a close. An absolute bargain in the first year of his new contract, Escobar's struggles in year two were both easy and hard to divine. The easy part: He just stopped hitting. The hard part: There's not a clear reason why. His average and max exit velos were similar to prior years, there wasn't a massive change in batted-ball profile, his walk and strikeout rates were comparable, heck even his hard-hit rate was almost exactly the same. The best tonic for both viewer and player was that the year came to a close. Next year brings a clean slate and plenty of motivation; Escobar will have much to prove in his walk year.

YEAR	TEAM	LVL	AGE	PA	DRC+	BABIP	BRR	FRAA	WARP
2018	MIN	MLB	29	408	115	.325	-0.1	3B(77): -2.1, SS(21): -0.0, 2B(1): 0.1	2.1
2018	ARI	MLB	29	223	113	.281	0.5	3B(54): -4.9	0.8
2019	ARI	MLB	30	699	116	.283	-0.6	3B(144): -8.4, 2B(33): 1.1	3.3
2020	ARI	MLB	31	222	84	.244	1.7	3B(47): 1.7, 2B(3): -0.1	0.2
2021 FS	ARI	MLB	32	600	94	.279	0.3	3B -1, 2B 0	0.7
2021 DC	ARI	MLB	32	543	94	.279	0.3	3B -1, 2B 0	0.6

Eduardo Escobar, continued

Batted Ball Distribution

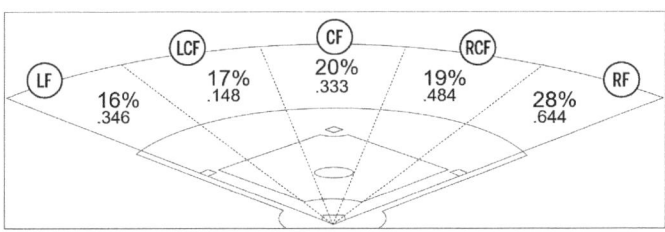

Strike Zone vs LHP   Strike Zone vs RHP

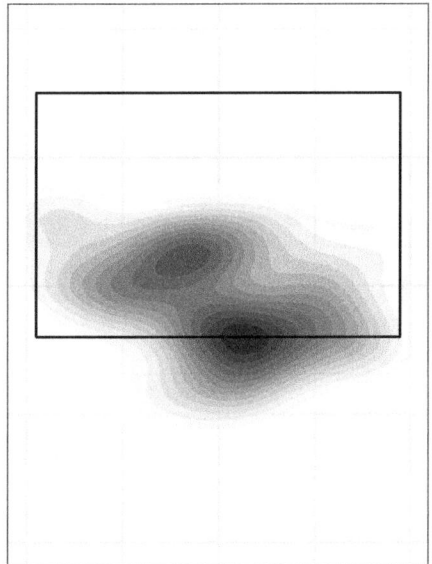

Arizona Diamondbacks 2021

Carson Kelly C
Born: 07/14/94   Age: 26   Bats: R   Throws: R
Height: 6'2"   Weight: 210   Origin: Round 2, 2012 Draft (#86 overall)

YEAR	TEAM	LVL	AGE	PA	R	2B	3B	HR	RBI	BB	K	SB	CS	AVG/OBP/SLG
2018	MEM	AAA	23	349	38	14	1	7	41	48	48	0	0	.269/.378/.395
2018	STL	MLB	23	42	1	0	0	0	3	3	7	0	0	.114/.205/.114
2019	ARI	MLB	24	365	46	19	0	18	47	48	79	0	0	.245/.348/.478
2020	ARI	MLB	25	129	11	5	0	5	19	6	29	0	0	.221/.264/.385
2021 FS	ARI	MLB	26	600	74	22	1	20	72	56	133	0	1	.236/.315/.397
2021 DC	ARI	MLB	26	404	50	15	1	13	48	38	90	0	0	.236/.315/.397

Comparables: Alex Avila, Josmil Pinto, Jim Pagliaroni

YEAR	TEAM	P. COUNT	FRM RUNS	BLK RUNS	THRW RUNS	TOT RUNS
2018	STL	1735	-0.8	-0.3	0.0	-1.1
2019	ARI	13169	-0.9	2.6	0.3	2.0
2020	ARI	4964	3.1	0.0	0.1	3.3
2021	ARI	13228	5.7	0.8	-0.8	5.6
2021	ARI	13228	5.7	-0.5	-0.8	4.3

Phoenix is one of the driest metro areas in the United States, though Las Vegas actually holds the title. Kelly took to the starting catcher role in 2019 like a duck to water, hitting more like a corner bat than a backstop. Fast forward a year, and his offensive production all but evaporated in the desert air. It's not just on the surface, either, as digging into his peripheral stats only supports the arid topline numbers. He'll spend the offseason looking for a more productive watering hole in the lineup, but if he can't find one in 2021, well, it's going to burn.

YEAR	TEAM	LVL	AGE	PA	DRC+	BABIP	BRR	FRAA	WARP
2018	MEM	AAA	23	349	113	.299	-0.6	C(83): 10.1, 1B(1): 0.0	2.8
2018	STL	MLB	23	42	74	.143	-0.2	C(16): -0.9	0.0
2019	ARI	MLB	24	365	115	.271	-1.2	C(101): -0.1, 3B(1): -0.0	2.5
2020	ARI	MLB	25	129	87	.250	-0.7	C(38): 0.5, P(1): -0.0	0.5
2021 FS	ARI	MLB	26	600	98	.277	-0.8	C 6, 1B 0	2.9
2021 DC	ARI	MLB	26	404	98	.277	-0.5	C 6	1.9

Carson Kelly, continued

Batted Ball Distribution

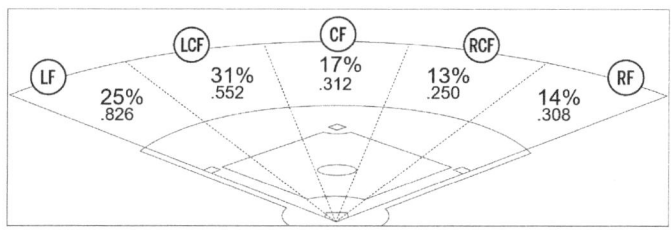

Strike Zone vs LHP   Strike Zone vs RHP

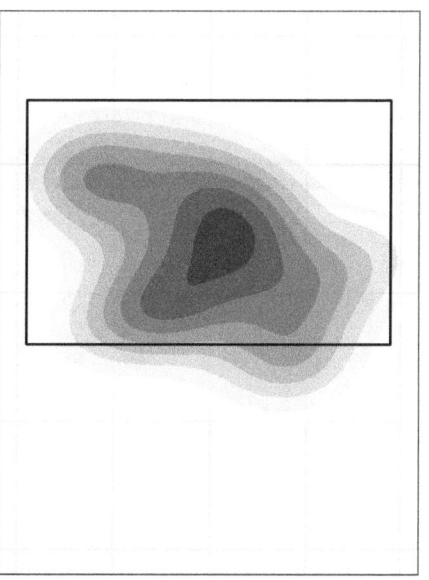

Type	Frequency	Velocity	H Movement	V Movement
● Fastball	100.0%	75 [44]	-7.5 [96]	-26.2 [69]

Arizona Diamondbacks 2021

Tim Locastro LF

Born: 07/14/92   Age: 28   Bats: R   Throws: R
Height: 6'1"   Weight: 195   Origin: Round 13, 2013 Draft (#385 overall)

YEAR	TEAM	LVL	AGE	PA	R	2B	3B	HR	RBI	BB	K	SB	CS	AVG/OBP/SLG
2018	OKC	AAA	25	356	61	23	2	4	25	28	52	18	2	.279/.389/.409
2018	LAD	MLB	25	14	6	1	0	0	0	2	5	4	0	.182/.357/.273
2019	RNO	AAA	26	143	35	11	2	8	21	10	24	9	1	.301/.394/.618
2019	ARI	MLB	26	250	38	12	2	1	17	14	44	17	0	.250/.357/.340
2020	ARI	MLB	27	82	15	4	1	2	7	8	14	4	0	.290/.395/.464
2021 FS	ARI	MLB	28	600	81	23	4	13	54	37	115	18	4	.249/.341/.387
2021 DC	ARI	MLB	28	428	58	16	3	9	39	26	82	12	3	.249/.341/.387

Comparables: Mike Huff, Felipe Crespo, Gene Stephens

Gimmicks are an age-old tradition in America. Buy this supplement and you'll lose 15 pounds! Put this in your gas tank and you'll get 10 percent more horsepower! If you call now, we'll include a second worthless piece of garbage for FREE! When it comes to Locastro, the gimmick is an obvious one. He was hit in nearly 10 percent of his plate appearances in 2019— practically a human bullseye. But that's a disservice to the sneaky skills that Locastro has developed. He's always been a threat on the bases, a capable outfielder at all three positions and has shown real growth at the plate. Locastro isn't a gimmick and neither is his game—he's a strong role player pushing for more.

YEAR	TEAM	LVL	AGE	PA	DRC+	BABIP	BRR	FRAA	WARP
2018	OKC	AAA	25	356	120	.327	4.2	CF(46): -3.7, 2B(30): -1.8, 1B(11): 0.6	1.5
2018	LAD	MLB	25	14	77	.333	0.4	CF(4): -0.1, LF(1): -0.0	0.0
2019	RNO	AAA	26	143	116	.319	1.9	CF(20): -1.4, RF(7): -0.2, LF(4): -0.4	0.7
2019	ARI	MLB	26	250	85	.310	0.3	LF(34): 1.6, RF(25): -0.0, CF(20): -1.9	0.2
2020	ARI	MLB	27	82	114	.340	-0.7	CF(13): 3.2, LF(7): -0.3, RF(6): -0.3	0.5
2021 FS	ARI	MLB	28	600	107	.296	1.2	CF 0, LF 1	2.6
2021 DC	ARI	MLB	28	428	107	.296	0.9	CF 0, LF 1	1.8

Tim Locastro, continued

Batted Ball Distribution

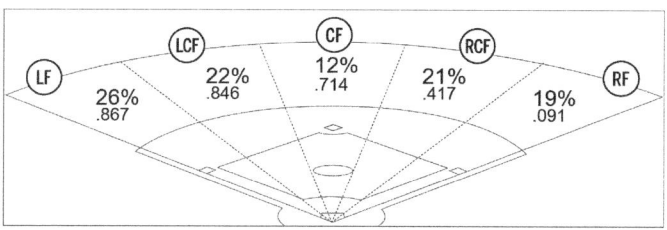

Strike Zone vs LHP   Strike Zone vs RHP

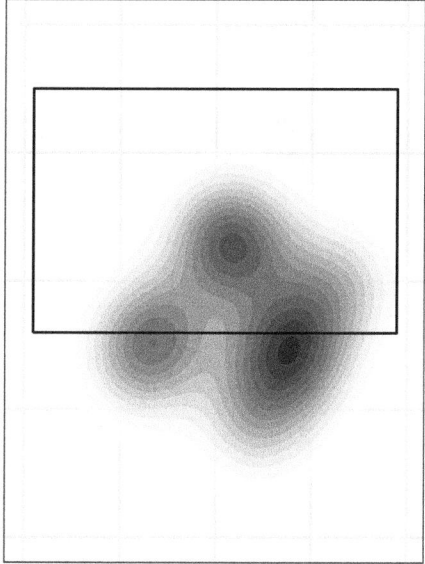

Ketel Marte 2B

Born: 10/12/93 Age: 27 Bats: S Throws: R
Height: 6'1" Weight: 210 Origin: International Free Agent, 2010

YEAR	TEAM	LVL	AGE	PA	R	2B	3B	HR	RBI	BB	K	SB	CS	AVG/OBP/SLG
2018	ARI	MLB	24	580	68	26	12	14	59	54	79	6	1	.260/.332/.437
2019	ARI	MLB	25	628	97	36	9	32	92	53	86	10	2	.329/.389/.592
2020	ARI	MLB	26	195	19	14	1	2	17	7	21	1	0	.287/.323/.409
2021 FS	ARI	MLB	27	600	85	30	6	17	69	45	90	7	3	.281/.340/.454
2021 DC	ARI	MLB	27	618	87	31	6	17	71	47	93	7	3	.281/.340/.454

Comparables: Jay Bell, Angel Berroa, Didi Gregorius

For three of the last four seasons, Marte has been a league-average hitter. It's just that the one outlier was, well, otherworldly. It'd be easy to call that outlying season just that—a blip on the radar. Marte notched fewer hard-hit balls in 2020, pulled the ball less often, hit it on the ground more, and registered his lowest power output since his rookie debut in 2015. The eye test, however, suggested that nothing much had changed from a season ago. Marte still swung like a tempest possessed his soul and the baseball was the sole object of his deepest aggressions. He still has an ability to do things that few others can, yet his produced outcomes changed in a way that surely cast uncertainty on the forecast.

YEAR	TEAM	LVL	AGE	PA	DRC+	BABIP	BRR	FRAA	WARP
2018	ARI	MLB	24	580	102	.282	0.6	2B(131): 4.5, SS(28): 1.8	2.9
2019	ARI	MLB	25	628	140	.342	1.9	CF(96): -8.3, 2B(83): -2.9, SS(11): -0.9	4.5
2020	ARI	MLB	26	195	101	.311	0.3	2B(41): 1.1, CF(3): -0.0, SS(2): -0.0	0.8
2021 FS	ARI	MLB	27	600	119	.309	0.5	2B 0, CF -1	3.2
2021 DC	ARI	MLB	27	618	119	.309	0.5	2B 0, CF -2	3.3

Ketel Marte, continued

Batted Ball Distribution

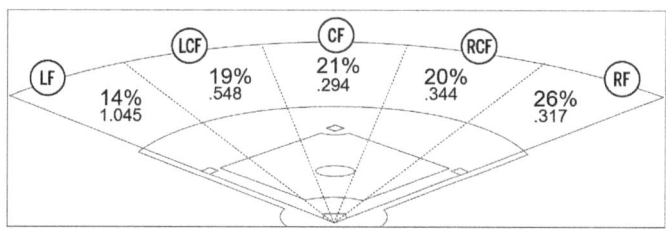

Strike Zone vs LHP   Strike Zone vs RHP

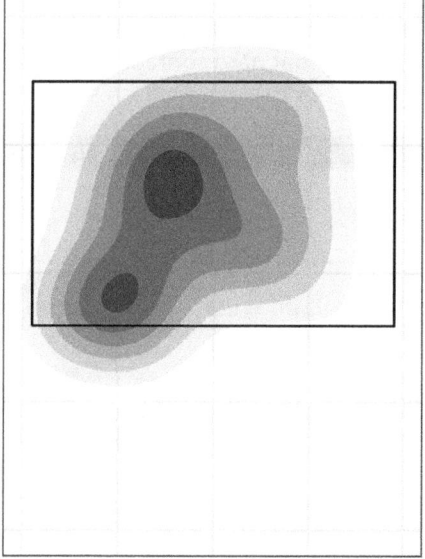

David Peralta LF

Born: 08/14/87 Age: 33 Bats: L Throws: L
Height: 6'1" Weight: 220 Origin: International Free Agent, 2005

YEAR	TEAM	LVL	AGE	PA	R	2B	3B	HR	RBI	BB	K	SB	CS	AVG/OBP/SLG
2018	ARI	MLB	30	614	75	25	5	30	87	48	124	4	0	.293/.352/.516
2019	ARI	MLB	31	423	48	29	3	12	57	35	87	0	0	.275/.343/.461
2020	ARI	MLB	32	218	19	10	1	5	34	13	45	1	0	.300/.339/.433
2021 FS	ARI	MLB	33	600	74	29	5	17	76	46	136	4	2	.263/.327/.431
2021 DC	ARI	MLB	33	582	72	28	5	16	73	44	132	4	2	.263/.327/.431

Comparables: Gary Ward, Matt Diaz, Kirk Gibson

What did the worms ever do to Peralta? They didn't ruin his pitching shoulder all those years ago. They didn't make the Cardinals cut him loose and they didn't relegate him to indy ball. All that toiling in obscurity, then the arduous journey to where he belonged in the first place ... what did the worms ever do to Peralta? They didn't keep him from running the bases like a locomotive. They didn't keep him from winning a Gold Glove, being named the defensive player of the year, or nabbing a Silver Slugger. What did the worms ever do to Peralta? They didn't keep him from developing a simple, powerful stroke from the left side, one that's wildly efficient. They didn't demand that he keep from launching that hard contact into the Arizona night sky. They didn't mandate the ground balls that hold back his game. What did the worms ever do to Peralta?

YEAR	TEAM	LVL	AGE	PA	DRC+	BABIP	BRR	FRAA	WARP
2018	ARI	MLB	30	614	121	.328	1.2	LF(138): -11.0, RF(5): -0.5	2.1
2019	ARI	MLB	31	423	96	.327	-2.8	LF(93): 13.4	2.0
2020	ARI	MLB	32	218	88	.361	-0.2	LF(45): 4.2	0.7
2021 FS	ARI	MLB	33	600	105	.322	0.2	LF 2, RF 0	2.1
2021 DC	ARI	MLB	33	582	105	.322	0.2	LF 2	1.9

David Peralta, continued

Batted Ball Distribution

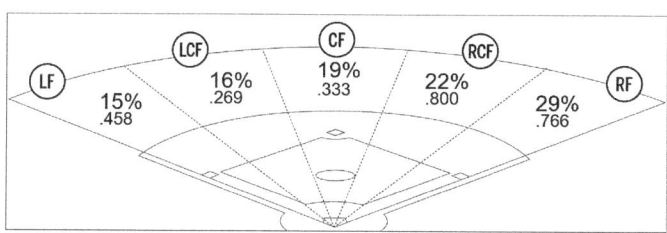

Strike Zone vs LHP   Strike Zone vs RHP

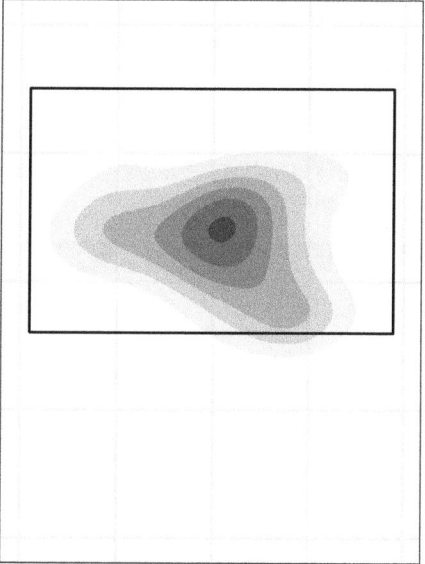

Diamondbacks Player Analysis - 29

Arizona Diamondbacks 2021

Josh Rojas 3B

Born: 06/30/94 Age: 27 Bats: L Throws: R
Height: 6'1" Weight: 200 Origin: Round 26, 2017 Draft (#781 overall)

YEAR	TEAM	LVL	AGE	PA	R	2B	3B	HR	RBI	BB	K	SB	CS	AVG/OBP/SLG
2018	FAY	HI-A	24	105	20	11	2	1	10	15	13	12	0	.311/.410/.511
2018	CC	AA	24	451	64	23	4	7	45	53	76	26	14	.251/.338/.385
2019	CC	AA	25	195	29	13	2	8	30	22	28	13	6	.322/.405/.561
2019	RR	AAA	25	244	49	16	3	12	39	30	36	19	4	.310/.402/.586
2019	RNO	AAA	25	40	11	4	1	3	14	5	6	1	0	.514/.575/.943
2019	ARI	MLB	25	157	17	7	0	2	16	18	41	4	2	.217/.312/.312
2020	ARI	MLB	26	70	9	0	0	0	2	7	16	1	1	.180/.257/.180
2021 FS	ARI	MLB	27	600	74	24	8	16	67	60	147	19	6	.235/.319/.408
2021 DC	ARI	MLB	27	172	21	7	2	4	19	17	42	5	2	.235/.319/.408

Comparables: Duane Walker, Charlie Manuel, James Mouton

When the Diamondbacks dealt Zack Greinke to the Astros, it wasn't Rojas who headlined the deal. He felt very much like a throw-in—he was a senior sign utility player who'd done some nice work in the minors, but nothing flashy. But when Rojas came to Phoenix he made an unexpected splash, thanks to some injuries that hit the big-league club. He hit .291/.350/.455 over his first 60 plate appearances and looked the part of a mostly outfielding utility man. The problem is, of course, that he hasn't hit a lick since. He's a fair defender in the outfield and can handle the infield, too, but that first impression certainly hasn't held up. Without more offense, it's hard to see how he weaves his way into regular playing time.

YEAR	TEAM	LVL	AGE	PA	DRC+	BABIP	BRR	FRAA	WARP
2018	FAY	HI-A	24	105	154	.355	0.1	2B(10): 1.0, 1B(7): -0.0, LF(3): -0.5	0.7
2018	CC	AA	24	451	106	.291	1.0	LF(36): 2.2, 3B(16): 2.3, 1B(13): 1.4	1.1
2019	CC	AA	25	195	179	.348	0.0	2B(30): 0.6, 1B(12): 0.8, 3B(2): -0.2	2.1
2019	RR	AAA	25	244	149	.325	2.1	2B(15): -1.5, SS(15): 0.9, LF(13): 1.4	2.8
2019	RNO	AAA	25	40	152	.577	-0.3	SS(2): -0.4, LF(2): -0.0, RF(2): 0.1	1.9
2019	ARI	MLB	25	157	76	.295	-1.7	LF(33): 2.7, RF(6): 0.0, 2B(1): 0.0	0.0
2020	ARI	MLB	26	70	73	.234	0.3	2B(8): -0.0, SS(2): -0.4, LF(1): -0.1	-0.1
2021 FS	ARI	MLB	27	600	97	.297	2.3	2B -1, SS 0	1.5
2021 DC	ARI	MLB	27	172	97	.297	0.6	2B 0, SS 0	0.5

Josh Rojas, continued

Batted Ball Distribution

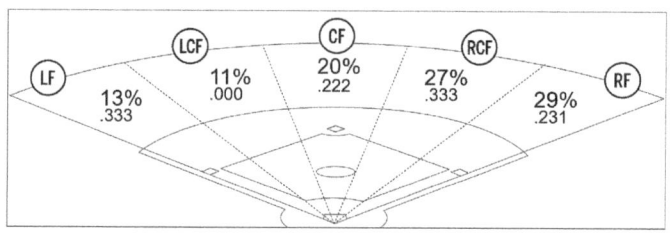

Strike Zone vs LHP   Strike Zone vs RHP

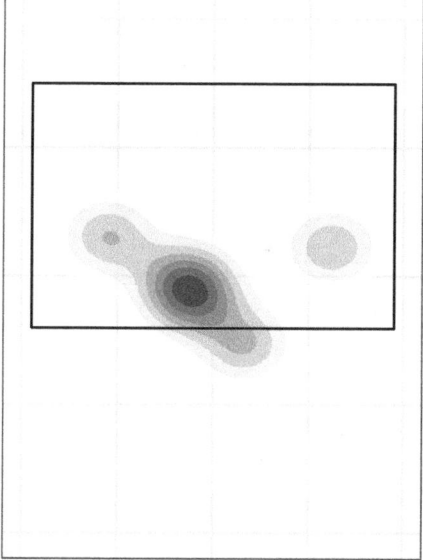

Daulton Varsho C

Born: 07/02/96 Age: 25 Bats: L Throws: R
Height: 5'10" Weight: 205 Origin: Round 2, 2017 Draft (#68 overall)

YEAR	TEAM	LVL	AGE	PA	R	2B	3B	HR	RBI	BB	K	SB	CS	AVG/OBP/SLG
2018	DIA	ROK	21	12	4	2	1	1	1	0	1	0	0	.500/.500/1.083
2018	VIS	HI-A	21	342	44	11	3	11	44	30	71	19	3	.286/.363/.451
2019	JXN	AA	22	452	85	25	4	18	58	42	63	21	5	.301/.378/.520
2020	ARI	MLB	23	115	16	5	2	3	9	12	33	3	1	.188/.287/.366
2021 FS	ARI	MLB	24	600	79	25	9	21	75	48	157	11	4	.249/.321/.450
2021 DC	ARI	MLB	24	448	59	19	6	16	56	36	117	8	3	.249/.321/.450

Comparables: Blake Swihart, Alex Avila, Tyler Stephenson

The Diamondbacks' highest-rated homegrown position player prospect to debut since Justin Upton didn't exactly put on a primetime show in the majors. His line was reminiscent of a backup catcher rather than that of a leading man. Billed as more than a catcher, he didn't disappoint in that regard. Varsho piled up more work in center field than he did behind the dish by a wide margin, highlighting his versatility while mostly looking the part in the field. One small hook on which to hang your hat? He did begin to look slightly more comfortable in his at-bats as the season progressed. Season One of The VarShow might not have met expectations, but don't sleep on Season Two.

YEAR	TEAM	LVL	AGE	PA	DRC+	BABIP	BRR	FRAA	WARP
2018	DIA	ROK	21	12		.500			
2018	VIS	HI-A	21	342	132	.341	2.5	C(55): 1.4	1.8
2019	JXN	AA	22	452	155	.317	5.9	C(76): -5.7, CF(4): -1.2	4.3
2020	ARI	MLB	23	115	87	.246	0.1	CF(14): 2.0, C(10): -0.1, LF(5): -0.1	0.3
2021 FS	ARI	MLB	24	600	107	.314	1.5	CF 8, C 0	4.0
2021 DC	ARI	MLB	24	448	107	.314	1.1	CF 6, C 0	2.5

Daulton Varsho, continued

Batted Ball Distribution

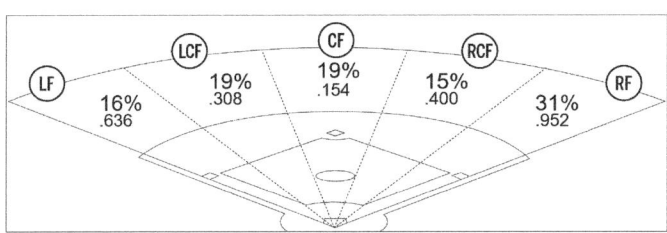

Strike Zone vs LHP   Strike Zone vs RHP

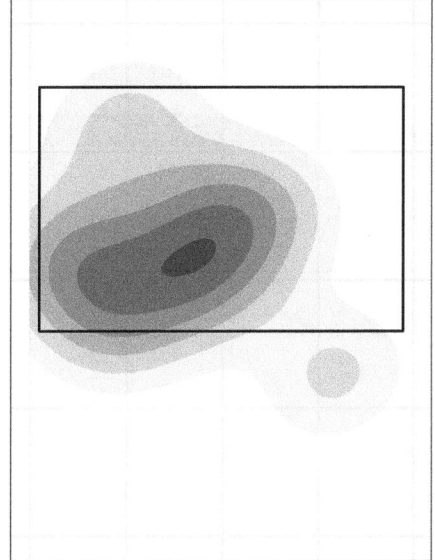

Christian Walker 1B

Born: 03/28/91 Age: 30 Bats: R Throws: R
Height: 6'0" Weight: 210 Origin: Round 4, 2012 Draft (#132 overall)

YEAR	TEAM	LVL	AGE	PA	R	2B	3B	HR	RBI	BB	K	SB	CS	AVG/OBP/SLG
2018	RNO	AAA	27	359	68	25	4	18	71	26	86	1	0	.299/.354/.568
2018	ARI	MLB	27	53	6	2	0	3	6	3	22	1	0	.163/.226/.388
2019	ARI	MLB	28	603	86	26	1	29	73	67	155	8	1	.259/.348/.476
2020	ARI	MLB	29	243	35	18	1	7	34	19	50	1	1	.271/.333/.459
2021 FS	ARI	MLB	30	600	77	26	3	24	83	52	152	2	1	.249/.322/.448
2021 DC	ARI	MLB	30	585	75	26	3	23	80	51	148	2	1	.249/.322/.448

Comparables: Tony Clark, Brian Daubach, Adam LaRoche

No one feels like cooking on Friday night. At the end of a long week the quickest route to relief and gratification is letting someone else cook for you. After this principle is embraced, the immediate question is whether one should dress up and go out, or order in from the comfort of their own sofa. Going out has its perks—virtually every option is available and one can get that fancy, special meal from that exclusive restaurant that'll make the friend group jealous. If Freddie Freeman is that fancy restaurant, Walker is more like In-N-Out (and not just because he's a Christian). Some think he's wildly overrated, others love what he brings to the table. Mostly, he gets the job done at a minimal cost.

YEAR	TEAM	LVL	AGE	PA	DRC+	BABIP	BRR	FRAA	WARP
2018	RNO	AAA	27	359	117	.351	-1.3	1B(64): 3.4, LF(18): -0.9	0.9
2018	ARI	MLB	27	53	58	.208	0.2	1B(7): 0.2, LF(1): -0.1	-0.1
2019	ARI	MLB	28	603	112	.312	1.7	1B(142): 10.8	3.1
2020	ARI	MLB	29	243	107	.317	0.1	1B(43): 3.1	0.9
2021 FS	ARI	MLB	30	600	111	.300	-0.5	1B 2, LF 0	2.0
2021 DC	ARI	MLB	30	585	111	.300	-0.4	1B 2	1.9

Christian Walker, continued

Batted Ball Distribution

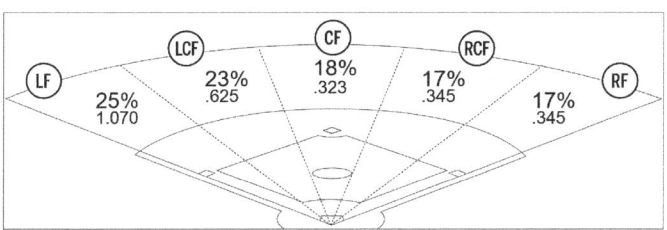

Strike Zone vs LHP   **Strike Zone vs RHP**

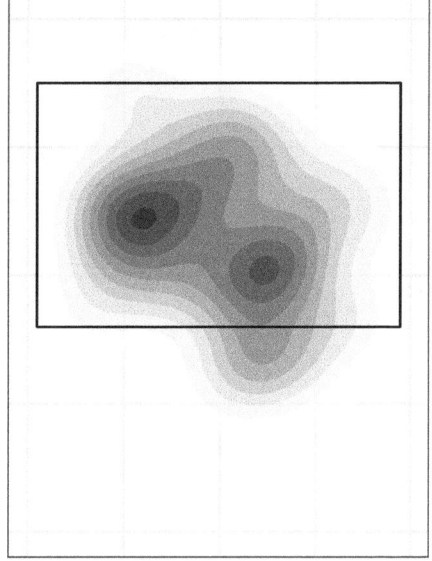

Travis Bergen   LHP

Born: 10/08/93   Age: 27   Bats: L   Throws: L
Height: 6'1"   Weight: 215   Origin: Round 7, 2015 Draft (#212 overall)

YEAR	TEAM	LVL	AGE	W	L	SV	G	GS	IP	H	HR	BB/9	K/9	K	GB%	BABIP
2018	DUN	HI-A	24	0	1	1	16	0	21	16	0	2.6	13.3	31	43.5%	.348
2018	NH	AA	24	4	1	7	27	0	35^2	26	2	2.3	10.9	43	37.0%	.270
2019	SAC	AAA	25	0	0	1	15	0	16^2	13	2	5.4	8.1	15	45.8%	.239
2019	SF	MLB	25	2	0	0	21	0	19^2	18	4	4.1	8.2	18	38.6%	.264
2020	ARI	MLB	26	1	0	1	8	0	8^1	5	1	9.7	11.9	11	43.8%	.267
2021 FS	ARI	MLB	27	2	2	0	57	0	50	44	7	4.0	10.1	55	40.4%	.289
2021 DC	ARI	MLB	27	2	2	0	51	0	46.7	41	6	4.0	10.1	52	40.4%	.289

Comparables: Aaron Bummer, Randy Rosario, Austin Davis

    Out with the old and in with the new(er). The Diamondbacks traded Andrew Chafin and filled his lefty specialist role with Bergen, for whom they traded Robbie Ray, at the 2020 trade deadline. The lefty can touch 95 mph but throwing strikes remains a challenge. He should get plenty of opportunities to rein it in this coming season..

YEAR	TEAM	LVL	AGE	WHIP	ERA	DRA-	WARP	MPH	FB%	WHF	CSP
2018	DUN	HI-A	24	1.05	1.71	73	0.3				
2018	NH	AA	24	0.98	0.50	62	0.8				
2019	SAC	AAA	25	1.38	3.78	87	0.3				
2019	SF	MLB	25	1.37	5.49	108	0.0	92.1	68.9%	17.8%	
2020	ARI	MLB	26	1.68	3.24	96	0.1	94.1	64.2%	26.7%	
2021 FS	ARI	MLB	27	1.33	4.04	96	0.3	92.9	67.0%	21.5%	44.3%
2021 DC	ARI	MLB	27	1.33	4.04	96	0.3	92.9	67.0%	21.5%	44.3%

Travis Bergen, continued

Pitch Shape vs LHH

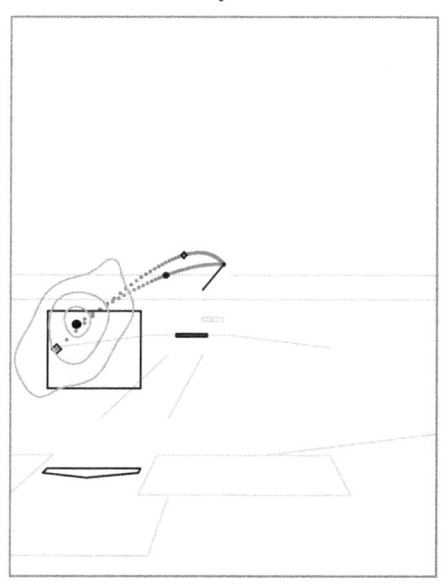

Pitch Shape vs RHH

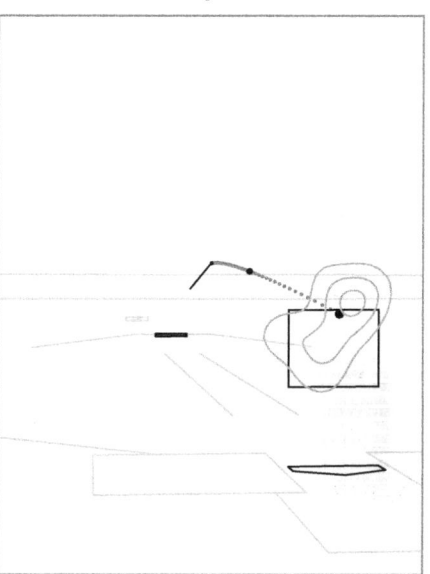

Type	Frequency	Velocity	H Movement	V Movement
● Fastball	64.2%	92.2 [99]	10.5 [82]	-14.8 [101]
◇ Curveball	35.2%	79.7 [104]	-7 [98]	-49.8 [97]

Madison Bumgarner LHP

Born: 08/01/89   Age: 31   Bats: R   Throws: L
Height: 6'4"   Weight: 255   Origin: Round 1, 2007 Draft (#10 overall)

YEAR	TEAM	LVL	AGE	W	L	SV	G	GS	IP	H	HR	BB/9	K/9	K	GB%	BABIP
2018	SF	MLB	28	6	7	0	21	21	129^2	118	14	3.0	7.6	109	42.1%	.277
2019	SF	MLB	29	9	9	0	34	34	207^2	191	30	1.9	8.8	203	35.2%	.292
2020	ARI	MLB	30	1	4	0	9	9	41^2	47	13	2.8	6.5	30	33.3%	.266
2021 FS	ARI	MLB	31	9	8	0	26	26	150	150	26	2.3	7.9	132	36.0%	.287
2021 DC	ARI	MLB	31	9	8	0	25	25	142.3	142	25	2.3	7.9	125	36.0%	.287

Comparables: Stephen Strasburg, Nathan Eovaldi, Kyle Hendricks

Yelp reviews are a dicey proposition. Sure, all people have bad opinions some of the time but, in the aggregate, there's often a shred of truth with enough accumulated perspectives. There's no denying the wisdom of the crowds, but it can be hard to tell if the majority has established a greater truth, or if it's just a bunch of nitpicky jerks. Finding signal amidst the noise on Bumgarner's season one, however, likely would take precious few submissions (be they novice reviewers or seasoned evaluators). The altered and delayed start of the 2020 season reportedly set him back as the veteran struggled with velocity, location and the health of his back, all of which kept him from repeating his familiar success. His hypothetical Yelp reviews would be sure to contain complaints about quality, quantity and cost. That's enough to put your local restaurant out of business instantly. The Diamondbacks, however, have four more years of Bumgarner on the menu. They might need to let customers know the dish comes pre-cooked.

YEAR	TEAM	LVL	AGE	WHIP	ERA	DRA-	WARP	MPH	FB%	WHF	CSP
2018	SF	MLB	28	1.24	3.26	99	1.3	92.2	34.4%	21.6%	
2019	SF	MLB	29	1.13	3.90	91	2.9	93.1	43.1%	24.7%	
2020	ARI	MLB	30	1.44	6.48	189	-1.6	89.8	39.9%	17.4%	
2021 FS	ARI	MLB	31	1.26	4.23	102	1.2	92.2	40.8%	22.7%	48.6%
2021 DC	ARI	MLB	31	1.26	4.23	102	1.2	92.2	40.8%	22.7%	48.6%

Madison Bumgarner, continued

Pitch Shape vs LHH

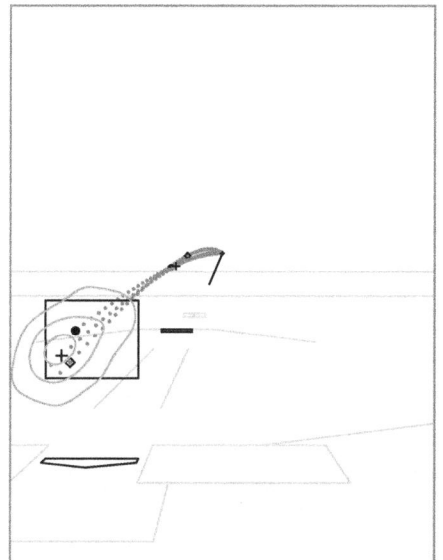

Pitch Shape vs RHH

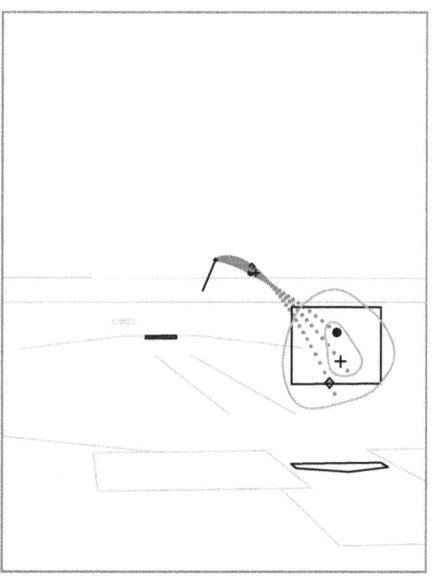

Type	Frequency	Velocity	H Movement	V Movement
● Fastball	39.1%	88.3 [87]	5.6 [106]	-16.3 [97]
+ Cutter	35.8%	83.5 [69]	-3.8 [112]	-28.7 [82]
◇ Curveball	22.4%	76.9 [93]	-9.9 [109]	-43.8 [110]

Humberto Castellanos   RHP

Born: 04/03/98   Age: 23   Bats: R   Throws: R
Height: 5'11"   Weight: 218   Origin: International Free Agent, 2015

YEAR	TEAM	LVL	AGE	W	L	SV	G	GS	IP	H	HR	BB/9	K/9	K	GB%	BABIP
2018	TRI	SS	20	0	0	1	2	0	2	1	0	0.0	9.0	2	100.0%	.200
2018	QC	LO-A	20	3	2	4	21	0	43	40	0	2.3	10.0	48	48.0%	.320
2019	QC	LO-A	21	3	0	4	14	0	36^1	29	4	1.5	11.4	46	43.6%	.281
2019	FAY	HI-A	21	1	1	3	15	0	25^2	30	1	2.1	9.5	27	62.5%	.377
2019	RR	AAA	21	0	1	0	5	0	12^2	4	1	2.1	7.1	10	53.3%	.103
2020	HOU	MLB	22	0	1	0	8	0	10^2	12	2	4.2	10.1	12	46.9%	.333
2021 FS	*ARI*	*MLB*	*23*	*2*	*2*	*0*	*57*	*0*	*50*	*48*	*7*	*3.2*	*8.3*	*45*	*45.2%*	*.290*
2021 DC	*ARI*	*MLB*	*23*	*1*	*1*	*0*	*31*	*0*	*26.7*	*25*	*3*	*3.2*	*8.3*	*24*	*45.2%*	*.290*

Comparables: Keone Kela, Trevor Gott, Patrick Sandoval

Castellanos brought the heat in one sense: by plunking Ramón Laureano, precipitating an extensive fracas and suspensions for Laureano and Astros coach Alex Cintrón. His low-90s fastball was considerably less fiery, but it surprisingly drew more whiffs than his other offerings, a sign that it's going to be hard for this arsenal to succeed long-term.

YEAR	TEAM	LVL	AGE	WHIP	ERA	DRA-	WARP	MPH	FB%	WHF	CSP
2018	TRI	SS	20	0.50	0.00	184	-0.1				
2018	QC	LO-A	20	1.19	2.09	60	1.0				
2019	QC	LO-A	21	0.96	3.22	69	0.6				
2019	FAY	HI-A	21	1.40	3.16	121	-0.4				
2019	RR	AAA	21	0.55	1.42	51	0.5				
2020	HOU	MLB	22	1.59	6.75	92	0.1	91.9	50.2%	21.9%	
2021 FS	*ARI*	*MLB*	*23*	*1.32*	*4.15*	*99*	*0.3*	*91.9*	*50.2%*	*21.9%*	*51.3%*
2021 DC	*ARI*	*MLB*	*23*	*1.32*	*4.15*	*99*	*0.1*	*91.9*	*50.2%*	*21.9%*	*51.3%*

Humberto Castellanos, continued

Pitch Shape vs LHH

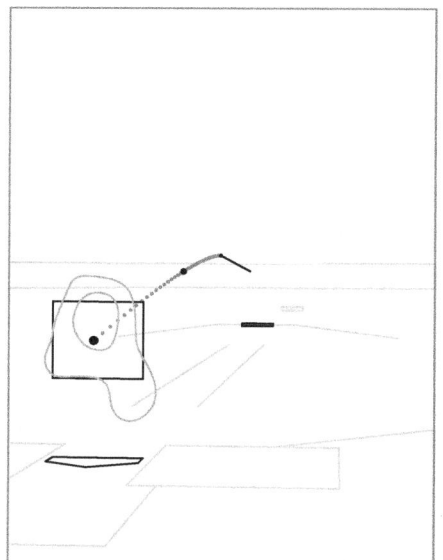

Pitch Shape vs RHH

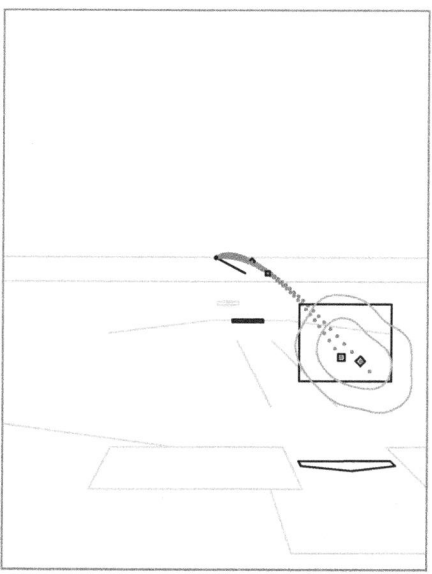

Type	Frequency	Velocity	H Movement	V Movement
● Fastball	31.4%	90.2 [93]	-7.2 [97]	-18.9 [89]
☐ Sinker	18.8%	89.4 [84]	-14.4 [90]	-27.8 [76]
▲ Changeup	14.0%	82.8 [91]	-11.9 [99]	-33.3 [84]
▽ Slider	9.7%	86.6 [112]	0.1 [81]	-25.2 [125]
◇ Curveball	26.1%	78.4 [99]	5.9 [93]	-41.2 [116]

Arizona Diamondbacks 2021

Taylor Clarke   RHP
Born: 05/13/93   Age: 28   Bats: R   Throws: R
Height: 6'4"   Weight: 220   Origin: Round 3, 2015 Draft (#76 overall)

YEAR	TEAM	LVL	AGE	W	L	SV	G	GS	IP	H	HR	BB/9	K/9	K	GB%	BABIP
2018	RNO	AAA	25	13	8	0	27	27	152	149	12	2.6	7.4	125	38.0%	.304
2019	VIS	HI-A	26	1	0	0	1	1	6	3	0	0.0	4.5	3	64.7%	.176
2019	RNO	AAA	26	3	1	0	8	8	36²	41	6	4.2	6.9	28	33.9%	.318
2019	ARI	MLB	26	5	5	1	23	15	84²	86	23	3.2	7.1	67	39.2%	.260
2020	ARI	MLB	27	3	0	0	12	5	43¹	35	8	4.4	8.3	40	44.3%	.237
2021 FS	ARI	MLB	28	9	9	0	26	26	150	144	25	3.5	8.0	134	39.9%	.280
2021 DC	ARI	MLB	28	6	5	0	47	9	70.3	67	12	3.5	8.0	62	39.9%	.280

Comparables: Buck Farmer, Robert Stephenson, Jeff Hoffman

The importance of hydration isn't lost on baseball players and critical liquids aren't just reserved for starters. Out in the bullpen, bottles of water, jugs of Gatorade and a carafe of coffee are standard fare. But Clarke was drinking something else in 2020. Some strange serum turned a lackluster Dr. Jekyll into a much more potent Mr. Hyde. Clarke was dubious again as a starting pitcher but batters managed just a .169/.272/.366 line off of him as a reliever. His ERA was a run and half better in relief and, while he didn't necessarily light the world on fire, he may have cemented his role going forward. The Diamondbacks have struggled to find consistency in the bullpen and Clarke looks to be part of the solution.

YEAR	TEAM	LVL	AGE	WHIP	ERA	DRA-	WARP	MPH	FB%	WHF	CSP
2018	RNO	AAA	25	1.27	4.03	92	2.2				
2019	VIS	HI-A	26	0.50	0.00	59	0.2				
2019	RNO	AAA	26	1.58	6.63	101	0.6				
2019	ARI	MLB	26	1.37	5.31	132	-0.7	95.3	53.2%	23.1%	
2020	ARI	MLB	27	1.29	4.36	105	0.3	95.3	45.5%	22.3%	
2021 FS	ARI	MLB	28	1.36	4.46	105	1.0	95.3	50.0%	22.8%	45.6%
2021 DC	ARI	MLB	28	1.36	4.46	105	0.3	95.3	50.0%	22.8%	45.6%

Taylor Clarke, continued

Pitch Shape vs LHH

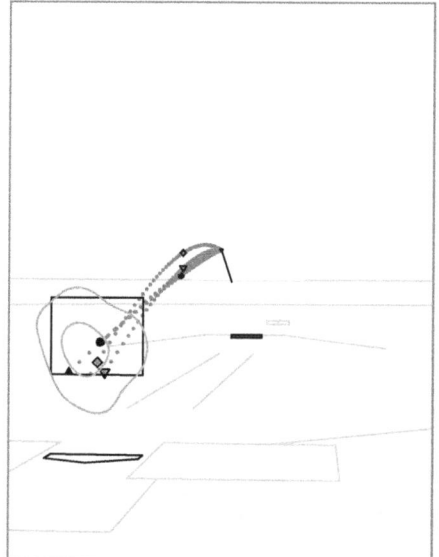

Pitch Shape vs RHH

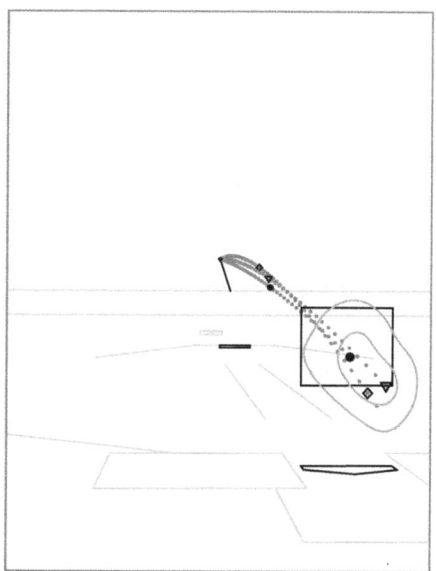

Type	Frequency	Velocity	H Movement	V Movement
● Fastball	44.9%	94.3 [105]	-4.8 [109]	-11.5 [110]
▲ Changeup	16.8%	88.8 [114]	-13 [93]	-25.1 [106]
▽ Slider	26.8%	86.3 [110]	4 [95]	-30.5 [110]
◇ Curveball	10.4%	79.9 [105]	4.8 [89]	-48.1 [101]

Arizona Diamondbacks 2021

Stefan Crichton RHP
Born: 02/29/92   Age: 29   Bats: R   Throws: R
Height: 6'3"   Weight: 205   Origin: Round 23, 2013 Draft (#699 overall)

YEAR	TEAM	LVL	AGE	W	L	SV	G	GS	IP	H	HR	BB/9	K/9	K	GB%	BABIP
2018	RNO	AAA	26	0	2	0	14	0	16	19	4	5.6	9.6	17	55.1%	.341
2019	RNO	AAA	27	4	3	1	36	0	57^1	52	4	2.4	8.2	52	57.9%	.300
2019	ARI	MLB	27	1	0	0	28	0	30^1	23	3	2.4	9.8	33	52.5%	.260
2020	ARI	MLB	28	2	2	5	26	0	26	22	1	3.1	8.0	23	47.9%	.292
2021 FS	ARI	MLB	29	2	2	7	57	0	50	47	6	2.7	8.4	46	48.8%	.294
2021 DC	ARI	MLB	29	2	2	7	57	0	60	57	7	2.7	8.4	56	48.8%	.294

Comparables: Kevin McCarthy, Juan Minaya, Shawn Armstrong

While a lost season for a franchise is a downer for just about everyone, it does present an opportunity for those at the fringes. Crichton is one of those guys. He entered the year firmly entrenched in the bullpen and navigated his way to the closer's role following Archie Bradley's move to Cincinnati. While his peripherals are fairly mundane, Crichton has shown a feel for avoiding opponents' barrels—in fact, he's only allowed four "barrels" per Statcast across 56 1/3 innings over the past two seasons. He'll need to keep that up because he doesn't miss the number of bats normally required of a bullpen anchor.

YEAR	TEAM	LVL	AGE	WHIP	ERA	DRA-	WARP	MPH	FB%	WHF	CSP
2018	RNO	AAA	26	1.81	10.12	78	0.3				
2019	RNO	AAA	27	1.17	3.61	50	2.1				
2019	ARI	MLB	27	1.02	3.56	76	0.5	94.5	63.6%	24.3%	
2020	ARI	MLB	28	1.19	2.42	89	0.4	93.7	61.4%	22.2%	
2021 FS	ARI	MLB	29	1.26	3.85	93	0.4	94.0	62.4%	23.1%	49.0%
2021 DC	ARI	MLB	29	1.26	3.85	93	0.5	94.0	62.4%	23.1%	49.0%

Stefan Crichton, continued

Pitch Shape vs LHH

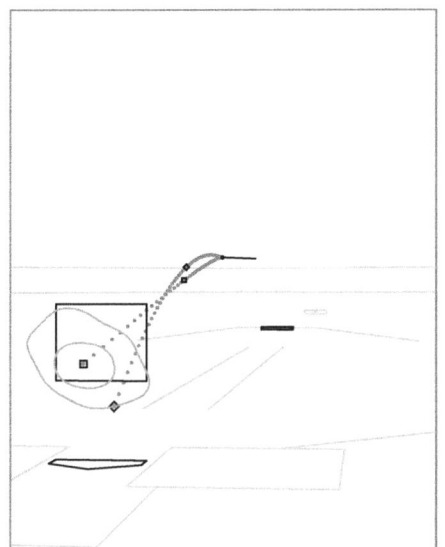

Pitch Shape vs RHH

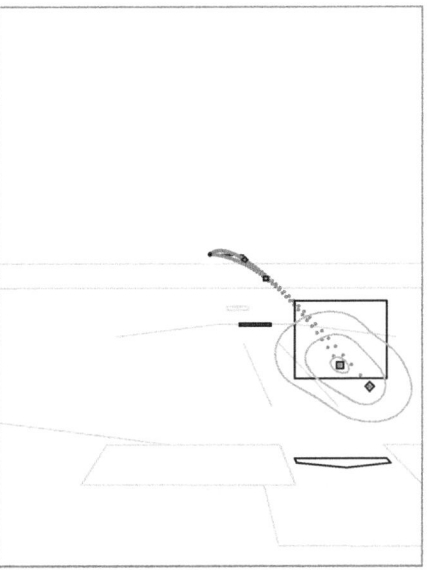

Type	Frequency	Velocity	H Movement	V Movement
☐ Sinker	58.2%	92.2 [99]	-15.6 [81]	-22 [95]
◇ Curveball	36.0%	77.8 [97]	12 [118]	-47.8 [101]

Arizona Diamondbacks 2021

Zac Gallen RHP
Born: 08/03/95   Age: 25   Bats: R   Throws: R
Height: 6'2"   Weight: 198   Origin: Round 3, 2016 Draft (#106 overall)

YEAR	TEAM	LVL	AGE	W	L	SV	G	GS	IP	H	HR	BB/9	K/9	K	GB%	BABIP
2018	NO	AAA	22	8	9	0	25	25	133¹	148	14	3.2	9.2	136	38.6%	.354
2019	NO	AAA	23	9	1	0	14	14	91¹	48	10	1.7	11.0	112	46.3%	.198
2019	ARI	MLB	23	2	3	0	8	8	43²	37	5	3.7	10.9	53	44.5%	.305
2019	MIA	MLB	23	1	3	0	7	7	36¹	25	3	4.5	10.7	43	34.1%	.259
2020	ARI	MLB	24	3	2	0	12	12	72	55	9	3.1	10.2	82	46.4%	.269
2021 FS	ARI	MLB	25	10	7	0	26	26	150	128	18	3.1	10.2	170	43.2%	.291
2021 DC	ARI	MLB	25	10	7	0	27	27	159.7	136	19	3.1	10.2	181	43.2%	.291

Comparables: José Berríos, Jack Flaherty, Jake Odorizzi

Biz Markie's career as a musician got off to an inauspicious start. His debut album dropped in 1988 and hardly anyone paid attention to "Goin' Off." The leading song on that album was titled, "Pickin' Boogers," and it should come as no surprise that few took notice. But a year later, things transformed for Markie. An odd, piano-laden rap dubbed, "Just a Friend" took the Billboard charts by storm. The song was everywhere. It holds two unique spots as both one of the greatest songs of hip-hop and also one of the most remarkable one-hit wonders ever. Gallen was born six years after "Just a Friend" hit the airwaves, and following a nifty bit of Bizness that sent Jazz Chisholm to the Marlins, he appears poised to be anything but a one-hit wonder—and could well end up the Markie acquisition of the Mike Hazen era. His sophomore effort proved that he's got staying power and won't be plummeting off the charts anytime soon.

YEAR	TEAM	LVL	AGE	WHIP	ERA	DRA-	WARP	MPH	FB%	WHF	CSP
2018	NO	AAA	22	1.47	3.65	79	2.8				
2019	NO	AAA	23	0.71	1.77	16	5.2				
2019	ARI	MLB	23	1.26	2.89	70	1.1	95.6	50.7%	30.2%	
2019	MIA	MLB	23	1.18	2.72	89	0.6	94.4	48.3%	28.5%	
2020	ARI	MLB	24	1.11	2.75	78	1.5	95.2	39.2%	30.4%	
2021 FS	ARI	MLB	25	1.20	3.29	82	3.0	95.3	43.9%	30.0%	43.7%
2021 DC	ARI	MLB	25	1.20	3.29	82	3.2	95.3	43.9%	30.0%	43.7%

Zac Gallen, continued

Pitch Shape vs LHH

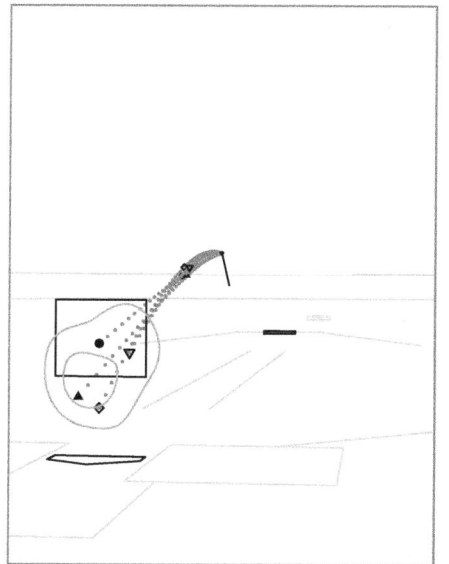

Pitch Shape vs RHH

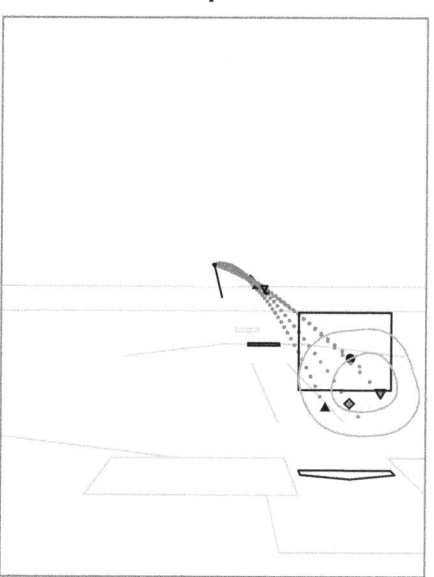

Type	Frequency	Velocity	H Movement	V Movement
● Fastball	38.9%	93.2 [102]	-3.2 [117]	-12.6 [107]
▲ Changeup	19.0%	84.8 [99]	-11.9 [99]	-31.3 [90]
▽ Slider	21.7%	87.8 [117]	5.5 [101]	-27.8 [117]
◇ Curveball	20.1%	81.4 [111]	5.9 [93]	-44.4 [109]

Arizona Diamondbacks 2021

Kevin Ginkel   RHP
Born: 03/24/94 Age: 27 Bats: L Throws: R
Height: 6'4" Weight: 235 Origin: Round 22, 2016 Draft (#659 overall)

YEAR	TEAM	LVL	AGE	W	L	SV	G	GS	IP	H	HR	BB/9	K/9	K	GB%	BABIP
2018	VIS	HI-A	24	1	1	4	20	0	27^1	20	2	1.0	13.2	40	36.1%	.310
2018	JXN	AA	24	5	0	5	34	0	42^2	26	3	1.9	12.7	60	35.9%	.264
2019	DIA	ROK	25	0	0	0	2	0	2	0	0	4.5	4.5	1	50.0%	.000
2019	JXN	AA	25	1	2	5	14	0	16^2	9	2	2.7	14.0	26	42.4%	.241
2019	RNO	AAA	25	1	0	6	15	0	16^2	10	2	4.3	19.4	36	39.1%	.381
2019	ARI	MLB	25	3	0	2	25	0	24^1	15	2	3.3	10.4	28	34.5%	.232
2020	ARI	MLB	26	0	2	1	19	0	16	21	3	7.3	10.1	18	29.2%	.400
2021 FS	ARI	MLB	27	2	2	5	57	0	50	41	6	4.0	11.3	62	35.9%	.290
2021 DC	ARI	MLB	27	2	2	5	57	0	60	49	8	4.0	11.3	75	35.9%	.290

Comparables: Kyle Crick, Phil Maton, Keone Kela

The old saw is that it's better to be lucky than good. It's a tautology, of course—true in any given moment that it's said, but with no regard for the instances surrounding it. It's stupid, is what we're trying to say. Being good is a repeatable skill. Being lucky ... less so. A year ago, Ginkel was probably more the former than the latter. His 2019 batting average on balls in play was leaner than a dinner on the Atkins diet. Last season, he went full Keto without reading the fine print. Turns out that being lucky or good is being spoiled for choice because Ginkel was neither. His ERA didn't dip below double-digits until his 12th appearance of the season in late August, and reached a season-low of 6.32 only briefly before he was optioned to the alternate site in mid-September. He'll have to try another diet in 2021.

YEAR	TEAM	LVL	AGE	WHIP	ERA	DRA-	WARP	MPH	FB%	WHF	CSP
2018	VIS	HI-A	24	0.84	0.99	48	0.8				
2018	JXN	AA	24	0.82	1.69	54	1.2				
2019	DIA	ROK	25	0.50	0.00						
2019	JXN	AA	25	0.84	2.16	49	0.4				
2019	RNO	AAA	25	1.08	1.62	31	0.8				
2019	ARI	MLB	25	0.99	1.48	78	0.4	95.3	54.0%	32.4%	
2020	ARI	MLB	26	2.12	6.75	119	0.0	97.0	59.7%	32.9%	
2021 FS	ARI	MLB	27	1.27	3.63	88	0.6	96.3	57.2%	32.7%	42.4%
2021 DC	ARI	MLB	27	1.27	3.63	88	0.7	96.3	57.2%	32.7%	42.4%

Kevin Ginkel, continued

Pitch Shape vs LHH

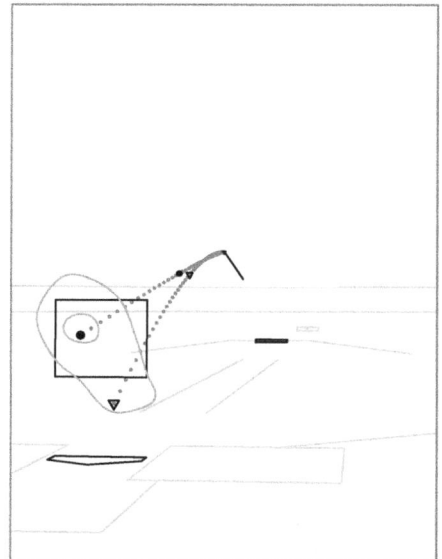

Pitch Shape vs RHH

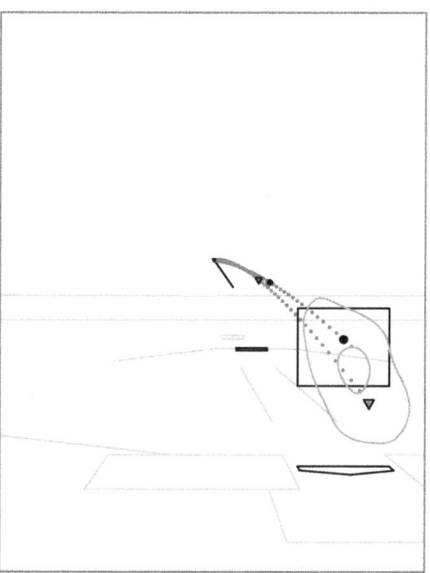

Type	Frequency	Velocity	H Movement	V Movement
● Fastball	58.3%	95.5 [109]	-9.2 [88]	-12.5 [108]
▽ Slider	38.5%	84 [100]	3 [92]	-35.7 [94]

Merrill Kelly RHP

Born: 10/14/88 Age: 32 Bats: R Throws: R
Height: 6'2" Weight: 210 Origin: Round 8, 2010 Draft (#251 overall)

YEAR	TEAM	LVL	AGE	W	L	SV	G	GS	IP	H	HR	BB/9	K/9	K	GB%	BABIP
2019	ARI	MLB	30	13	14	0	32	32	183^1	184	29	2.8	7.8	158	41.9%	.294
2020	ARI	MLB	31	3	2	0	5	5	31^1	26	5	1.4	8.3	29	45.6%	.247
2021 FS	ARI	MLB	32	9	8	0	26	26	150	144	23	3.0	8.2	135	42.9%	.286
2021 DC	ARI	MLB	32	7	6	0	22	21	111.3	107	17	3.0	8.2	101	42.9%	.286

Comparables: Rick Porcello, Ian Kennedy, Ervin Santana

It took Kelly nine years from the time he was drafted to make the majors. That includes five years in the minors and four in Korea, where he was good enough to earn a two-year major-league pact from the Diamondbacks. He soaked up innings at the back of the rotation in 2019, and when more was asked of him heading into 2020, he was up to the task ... through five starts. Baseball is cruel, and what took nine years (and then some) to achieve has been imperiled in the flash of an eye: Kelly required surgery to address thoracic outlet syndrome. The recovery from that surgery is fraught, and the results for those who do come back haven't been inspiring. According to research by FanGraphs' Jay Jaffe, only five pitchers since 2001 have returned to produce better ERA- totals post-surgery than prior to going under the knife. It's a tough blow for a player whose performance laid the groundwork for others like Josh Lindblom and Chris Flexen to reimagine their big-league careers after stints in Korea.

YEAR	TEAM	LVL	AGE	WHIP	ERA	DRA-	WARP	MPH	FB%	WHF	CSP
2019	ARI	MLB	30	1.31	4.42	101	1.6	94.1	65.4%	22.4%	
2020	ARI	MLB	31	0.99	2.59	87	0.5	93.9	65.5%	23.5%	
2021 FS	ARI	MLB	32	1.30	4.05	98	1.6	94.0	65.5%	22.6%	49.4%
2021 DC	ARI	MLB	32	1.30	4.05	98	1.2	94.0	65.5%	22.6%	49.4%

Merrill Kelly, continued

Pitch Shape vs LHH

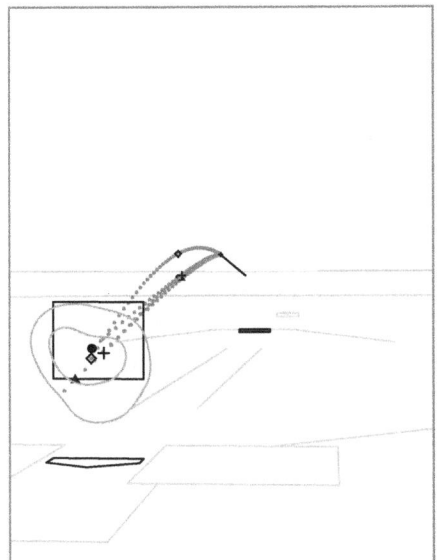

Pitch Shape vs RHH

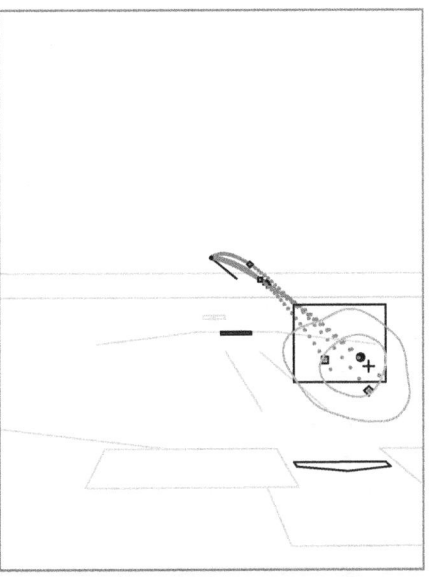

Type	Frequency	Velocity	H Movement	V Movement
● Fastball	26.3%	92.2 [99]	-5.2 [107]	-14.7 [101]
☐ Sinker	20.2%	91.3 [94]	-14.3 [91]	-22.7 [93]
+ Cutter	18.7%	90.7 [115]	-0.1 [87]	-18.1 [124]
▲ Changeup	12.2%	87.3 [108]	-14.7 [84]	-26.9 [102]
◇ Curveball	22.1%	81.2 [110]	8.5 [104]	-47.6 [102]

Yoan López   RHP

Born: 01/02/93   Age: 28   Bats: R   Throws: R
Height: 6'3"   Weight: 205   Origin: International Free Agent, 2015

YEAR	TEAM	LVL	AGE	W	L	SV	G	GS	IP	H	HR	BB/9	K/9	K	GB%	BABIP
2018	JXN	AA	25	2	6	12	45	0	61²	38	4	3.8	12.7	87	35.3%	.260
2018	ARI	MLB	25	0	0	0	10	0	9	7	2	1.0	11.0	11	52.2%	.250
2019	ARI	MLB	26	2	7	1	70	0	60²	52	11	2.5	6.2	42	43.3%	.234
2020	ARI	MLB	27	0	1	0	20	0	19²	21	4	4.1	7.3	16	54.8%	.293
2021 FS	ARI	MLB	28	2	2	0	57	0	50	47	7	3.6	8.6	47	44.2%	.289
2021 DC	ARI	MLB	28	2	2	0	57	0	53.3	50	8	3.6	8.6	50	44.2%	.289

Comparables: Mike Mayers, John Curtiss, Archie Bradley

You could see it coming, couldn't you? In 2019, López got damn lucky. He outperformed his ERA by almost two full runs according to DRA and, night after night, got away with fat fastballs and hanging sliders that managed, somehow, to repeatedly go unpunished. That's not to say his stuff was so filthy that it couldn't be hit. It often was hit, and hit hard, but hit right at a defender again and again. Regression is a you-know-what and it caught up with him in 2020 in a very predictable, debilitating way. The once-prized Cuban has a flat fastball that he can't throw carefully enough for strikes to get to his decent slider. He's running out of leash and, without some improvement, 2021 could be his swan song in the desert.

YEAR	TEAM	LVL	AGE	WHIP	ERA	DRA-	WARP	MPH	FB%	WHF	CSP
2018	JXN	AA	25	1.04	2.92	58	1.6				
2018	ARI	MLB	25	0.89	3.00	85	0.1	98.5	67.2%	28.8%	
2019	ARI	MLB	26	1.14	3.41	106	0.1	98.1	57.1%	21.3%	
2020	ARI	MLB	27	1.53	5.95	102	0.2	96.9	54.7%	25.2%	
2021 FS	ARI	MLB	28	1.35	4.24	101	0.2	97.7	56.8%	22.8%	48.3%
2021 DC	ARI	MLB	28	1.35	4.24	101	0.2	97.7	56.8%	22.8%	48.3%

Yoan López, continued

Pitch Shape vs LHH

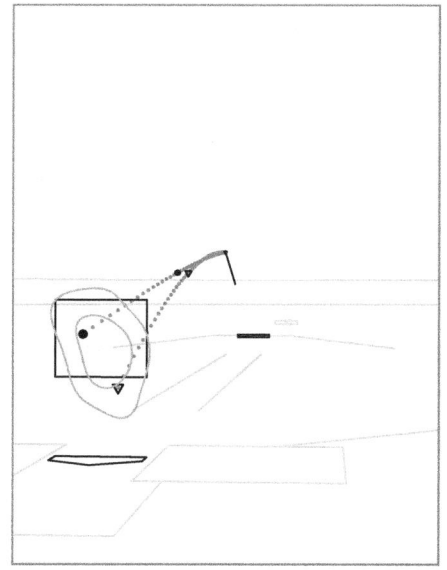

Pitch Shape vs RHH

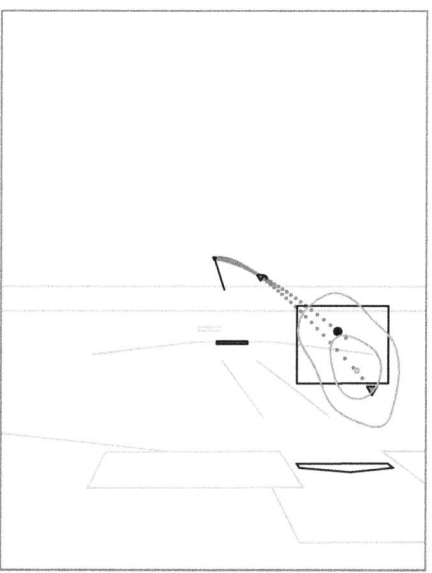

Type	Frequency	Velocity	H Movement	V Movement
● Fastball	53.1%	95.3 [109]	-3.8 [114]	-13.3 [105]
▽ Slider	43.9%	85.7 [108]	5.5 [101]	-34.6 [97]

Arizona Diamondbacks 2021

Humberto Mejía   RHP
Born: 03/03/97   Age: 24   Bats: R   Throws: R
Height: 6'4"   Weight: 235   Origin: International Free Agent, 2013

YEAR	TEAM	LVL	AGE	W	L	SV	G	GS	IP	H	HR	BB/9	K/9	K	GB%	BABIP
2018	BAT	SS	21	1	6	0	15	12	62²	55	8	2.0	8.5	59	36.9%	.275
2019	CLI	LO-A	22	5	1	1	13	10	66²	42	4	2.6	9.2	68	32.7%	.229
2019	JUP	HI-A	22	0	1	0	5	4	23²	15	2	1.9	8.0	21	43.8%	.210
2020	MIA	MLB	23	0	2	0	3	3	10	13	3	5.4	9.9	11	29.0%	.357
2021 FS	ARI	MLB	24	2	3	0	57	0	50	49	8	3.4	8.0	44	36.0%	.287
2021 DC	ARI	MLB	24	0	0	0	3	3	12.7	12	2	3.4	8.0	11	36.0%	.287

Comparables: Joe Musgrove, David Paulino, Beau Burrows

Part of the Starling Marté return, Mejía made his big-league debut in 2020 out of pure necessity. A virus-ravaged Miami squad turned to him in a pinch, then dealt him to the Diamondbacks where his arsenal likely fits best in a relief role.

YEAR	TEAM	LVL	AGE	WHIP	ERA	DRA-	WARP	MPH	FB%	WHF	CSP
2018	BAT	SS	21	1.10	3.30	113	0.0				
2019	CLI	LO-A	22	0.92	2.02	55	1.9				
2019	JUP	HI-A	22	0.85	2.28	63	0.5				
2020	MIA	MLB	23	1.90	5.40	115	0.0	94.0	52.2%	22.0%	
2021 FS	ARI	MLB	24	1.37	4.51	106	0.1	94.0	52.2%	22.0%	46.6%
2021 DC	ARI	MLB	24	1.37	4.51	106	0.1	94.0	52.2%	22.0%	46.6%

Humberto Mejía, continued

Pitch Shape vs LHH

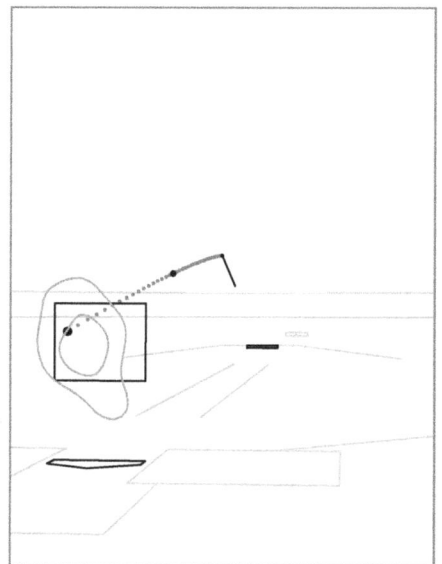

Pitch Shape vs RHH

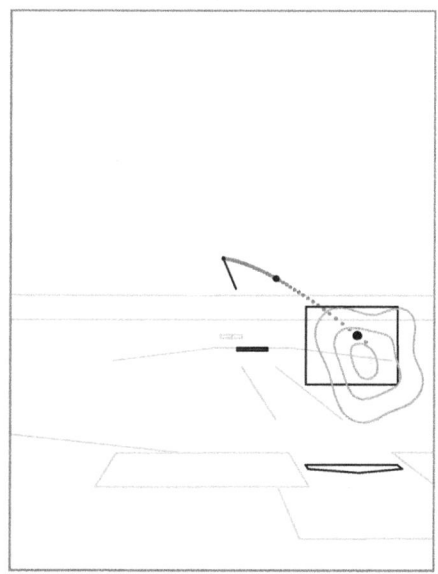

Type	Frequency	Velocity	H Movement	V Movement
● Fastball	52.2%	93 [101]	-6.2 [102]	-12.4 [108]
▲ Changeup	9.8%	86.1 [104]	-11.1 [103]	-23.8 [110]
▽ Slider	17.1%	84.4 [102]	5.2 [100]	-32.5 [104]
◇ Curveball	21.0%	78.8 [101]	5.3 [91]	-43.6 [111]

Caleb Smith LHP

Born: 07/28/91   Age: 29   Bats: R   Throws: L
Height: 6'0"   Weight: 206   Origin: Round 14, 2013 Draft (#434 overall)

YEAR	TEAM	LVL	AGE	W	L	SV	G	GS	IP	H	HR	BB/9	K/9	K	GB%	BABIP
2018	MIA	MLB	26	5	6	0	16	16	77^1	63	10	3.8	10.2	88	28.2%	.279
2019	JAX	AA	27	0	0	0	2	2	9^1	7	4	1.9	18.3	19	25.0%	.250
2019	MIA	MLB	27	10	11	0	28	28	153^1	128	33	3.5	9.9	168	26.0%	.252
2020	ARI	MLB	28	0	0	0	5	4	14	6	3	7.7	9.6	15	27.3%	.100
2021 FS	ARI	MLB	29	9	8	0	26	26	150	125	25	4.1	10.3	171	29.9%	.272
2021 DC	ARI	MLB	29	5	6	0	25	25	77.7	65	13	4.1	10.3	88	29.9%	.272

Comparables: Steven Brault, Austin Brice, Marco Gonzales

There's a dirty little secret that's rarely whispered and almost certainly never spoken aloud: Some of Dave Stewart's trades were alright. Take, for example, the one that netted the Diamondbacks left-hander Robbie Ray. For a few years there, Ray was quite valuable and, often, a dominant-if-flawed starting pitcher. When he wasn't on, he was still able to rack up strikeouts but walked too many and was prone to the long ball. Smith isn't wholly dissimilar in that the free passes and dingers can pile up on him without the elite strikeout numbers. Will a return to full health and a change of scenery do him well? That's the gamble Hazen is making. If he's right, the Marlins might have to stop picking up his calls, because between Zac Gallen and Smith they'll have given up 40 percent of a starting rotation.

YEAR	TEAM	LVL	AGE	WHIP	ERA	DRA-	WARP	MPH	FB%	WHF	CSP
2018	MIA	MLB	26	1.24	4.19	90	1.1	94.3	59.1%	27.4%	
2019	JAX	AA	27	0.96	5.79	58	0.2				
2019	MIA	MLB	27	1.23	4.52	93	2.0	93.5	53.7%	28.0%	
2020	ARI	MLB	28	1.29	2.57	134	-0.1	93.4	51.3%	35.4%	
2021 FS	ARI	MLB	29	1.29	3.98	95	1.8	93.7	54.5%	28.6%	47.2%
2021 DC	ARI	MLB	29	1.29	3.98	95	0.9	93.7	54.5%	28.6%	47.2%

Caleb Smith, continued

Pitch Shape vs LHH

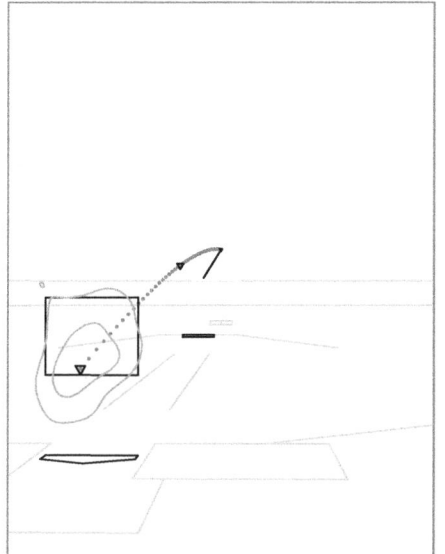

Pitch Shape vs RHH

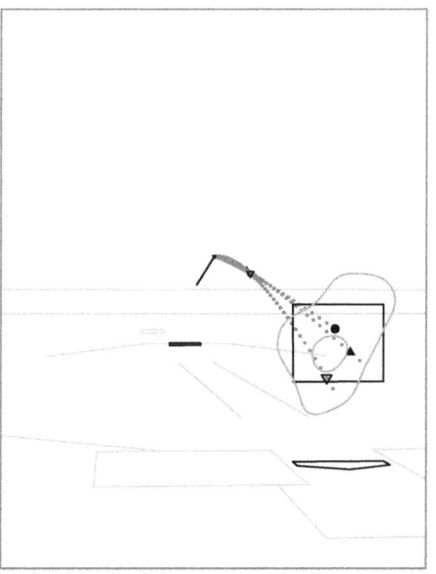

Type	Frequency	Velocity	H Movement	V Movement
● Fastball	51.3%	92 [98]	9.3 [88]	-12.4 [108]
▲ Changeup	14.6%	81.7 [87]	12.2 [97]	-24.5 [108]
▽ Slider	26.6%	83.4 [97]	-3.2 [92]	-32.3 [104]
◇ Curveball	7.5%	77.1 [94]	-5.5 [92]	-45.8 [106]

Riley Smith RHP

Born: 01/15/95   Age: 26   Bats: R   Throws: R
Height: 6'1"   Weight: 175   Origin: Round 24, 2016 Draft (#719 overall)

YEAR	TEAM	LVL	AGE	W	L	SV	G	GS	IP	H	HR	BB/9	K/9	K	GB%	BABIP
2018	VIS	HI-A	23	8	6	0	26	25	151^1	141	15	2.9	8.8	148	48.2%	.310
2019	JXN	AA	24	4	4	0	13	13	71^1	65	4	2.0	7.8	62	48.6%	.298
2019	RNO	AAA	24	2	2	0	12	12	62^2	85	15	2.9	6.9	48	41.7%	.352
2020	ARI	MLB	25	2	0	0	6	0	18^1	15	1	2.5	8.8	18	46.8%	.311
2021 FS	*ARI*	*MLB*	*26*	*2*	*2*	*1*	*57*	*0*	*50*	*49*	*6*	*2.7*	*7.7*	*42*	*45.0%*	*.292*
2021 DC	*ARI*	*MLB*	*26*	*2*	*2*	*1*	*57*	*0*	*53.3*	*53*	*7*	*2.7*	*7.7*	*45*	*45.0%*	*.292*

Comparables: Tyler Wilson, Dillon Tate, Michael King

  The latter portion of the 2020 season provided few cheering opportunities for Diamondbacks fans, but Smith provided some moments to smile about. Long relief suited the contact-oriented, strike-throwing righty. A similar role may await him in 2021.

YEAR	TEAM	LVL	AGE	WHIP	ERA	DRA-	WARP	MPH	FB%	WHF	CSP
2018	VIS	HI-A	23	1.25	3.57	80	2.4				
2019	JXN	AA	24	1.14	2.27	80	0.9				
2019	RNO	AAA	24	1.68	6.89	141	-0.1				
2020	ARI	MLB	25	1.09	1.47	85	0.3	95.3	62.8%	13.9%	
2021 FS	*ARI*	*MLB*	*26*	*1.29*	*3.98*	*96*	*0.4*	*95.3*	*62.8%*	*13.9%*	*53.5%*
2021 DC	*ARI*	*MLB*	*26*	*1.29*	*3.98*	*96*	*0.4*	*95.3*	*62.8%*	*13.9%*	*53.5%*

Riley Smith, continued

Pitch Shape vs LHH

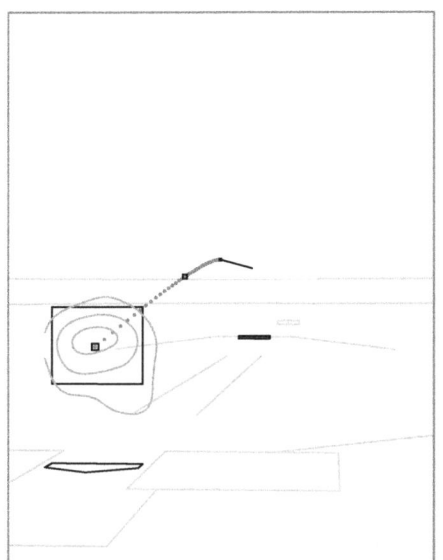

Pitch Shape vs RHH

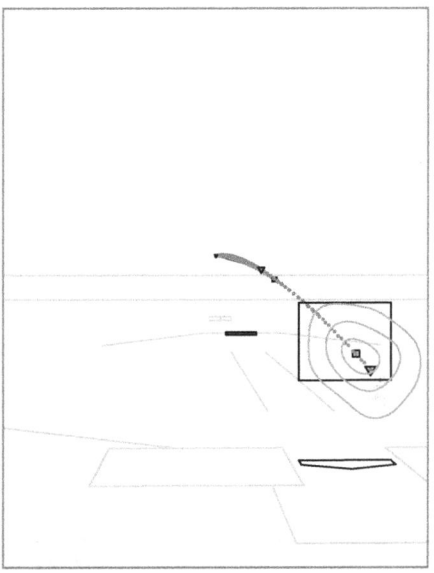

Type	Frequency	Velocity	H Movement	V Movement
☐ Sinker	62.8%	93.2 [104]	-11.6 [111]	-19.3 [104]
▽ Slider	18.0%	83 [96]	2.8 [91]	-34.2 [99]
◇ Curveball	18.0%	80.8 [109]	4.7 [88]	-47.2 [103]

Joakim Soria   RHP

Born: 05/18/84   Age: 37   Bats: R   Throws: R
Height: 6'3"   Weight: 208   Origin: International Free Agent, 2001

YEAR	TEAM	LVL	AGE	W	L	SV	G	GS	IP	H	HR	BB/9	K/9	K	GB%	BABIP
2018	CHW	MLB	34	0	3	16	40	0	38^2	35	2	2.3	11.4	49	32.7%	.327
2018	MIL	MLB	34	3	1	0	26	0	22	18	2	2.5	10.6	26	43.1%	.286
2019	OAK	MLB	35	2	4	1	71	1	69	51	9	2.6	10.3	79	37.5%	.253
2020	OAK	MLB	36	2	2	2	22	0	22^1	18	1	4.0	9.7	24	29.0%	.279
2021 FS	ARI	MLB	37	2	2	23	57	0	50	43	6	3.1	9.6	53	38.0%	.287
2021 DC	ARI	MLB	37	3	3	23	69	0	60	52	7	3.1	9.6	64	38.0%	.287

Comparables: Tom Henke, Sergio Romo, Lee Smith

Everything trended in the wrong direction for Soria in 2020—strikeout, walk and hit rates; exit velocity; and DRA, by which he had the second-worst season of his career. At 35, the age has been trending in the wrong direction for some time. The ERA was right, though, coming in below the mark Soria's established across 15 seasons. When someone's been around this long, oftentimes you have all the signs you need. Regardless of advanced metrics, the Soria of 2020 looked the same as in previous seasons by velocity and by results. With the journeyman hitting the open market again, teams will gravitate toward the results Soria has a career-long track record of providing.

YEAR	TEAM	LVL	AGE	WHIP	ERA	DRA-	WARP	MPH	FB%	WHF	CSP
2018	CHW	MLB	34	1.16	2.56	52	1.1	94.3	63.0%	30.8%	
2018	MIL	MLB	34	1.09	4.09	65	0.5	94.4	71.2%	26.2%	
2019	OAK	MLB	35	1.03	4.30	71	1.4	94.6	68.2%	28.9%	
2020	OAK	MLB	36	1.25	2.82	96	0.3	94.4	65.5%	23.5%	
2021 FS	ARI	MLB	37	1.22	3.44	85	0.7	94.5	66.9%	27.5%	49.4%
2021 DC	ARI	MLB	37	1.22	3.44	85	0.8	94.5	66.9%	27.5%	49.4%

Joakim Soria, continued

Pitch Shape vs LHH

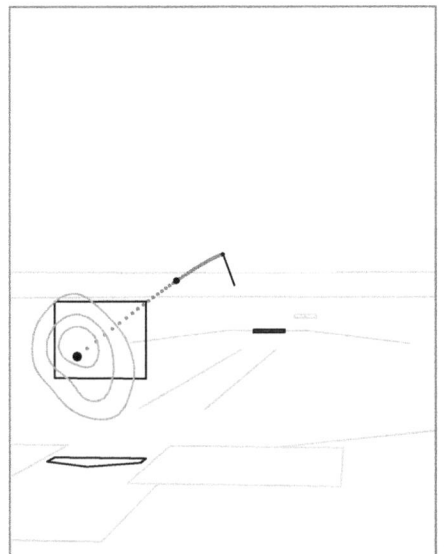

Pitch Shape vs RHH

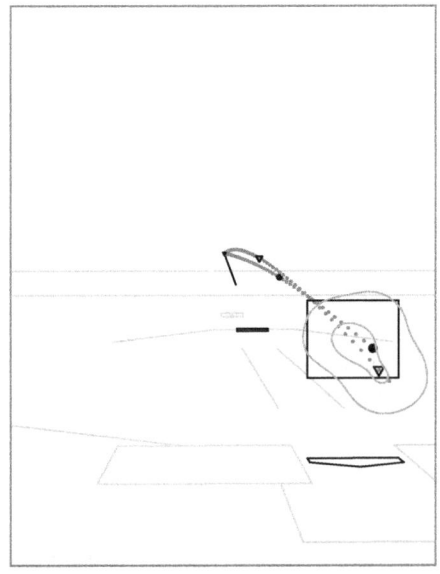

Type	Frequency	Velocity	H Movement	V Movement
● Fastball	64.0%	92.5 [100]	-5.1 [108]	-13.4 [105]
✕ Splitter	9.3%	87.2 [109]	-7.6 [101]	-25.9 [112]
▽ Slider	16.6%	78.1 [74]	13.7 [132]	-46.1 [64]
◇ Curveball	7.8%	72.5 [76]	11.4 [116]	-62.1 [69]

Arizona Diamondbacks 2021

Luke Weaver RHP
Born: 08/21/93   Age: 27   Bats: R   Throws: R
Height: 6'2"   Weight: 185   Origin: Round 1, 2014 Draft (#27 overall)

YEAR	TEAM	LVL	AGE	W	L	SV	G	GS	IP	H	HR	BB/9	K/9	K	GB%	BABIP
2018	STL	MLB	24	7	11	0	30	25	136¹	150	19	3.6	8.0	121	41.8%	.325
2019	ARI	MLB	25	4	3	0	12	12	64¹	55	6	2.0	9.7	69	40.8%	.292
2020	ARI	MLB	26	1	9	0	12	12	52	63	10	3.1	9.5	55	32.7%	.349
2021 FS	ARI	MLB	27	9	8	0	26	26	150	137	21	3.0	9.5	158	37.4%	.292
2021 DC	ARI	MLB	27	7	6	0	24	22	113.3	104	16	3.0	9.5	119	37.4%	.292

Comparables: Kevin Gausman, José Berríos, Jake Odorizzi

You've had a long week. A long several weeks, really. But it's Friday and it's time to shine, cut loose, change things up, and bring the heat. Only one problem—your wardrobe isn't complying and insists on throwing you a curveball. Nothing you want to wear is clean but instead soiled and tarnished ever so slightly. So you go digging through your closet and find that designer shirt you never wear. It's not that old and it was purchased with the promise of making you look both smart and cool. But every time you slip it on there's just something that doesn't work. No good with denim, no good with khaki. It's too soon to throw it out, so back on the hanger it goes to be deployed at a later date with hopefully, somehow, better results.

YEAR	TEAM	LVL	AGE	WHIP	ERA	DRA-	WARP	MPH	FB%	WHF	CSP
2018	STL	MLB	24	1.50	4.95	103	1.1	95.8	57.7%	22.4%	
2019	ARI	MLB	25	1.07	2.94	73	1.5	96.2	52.1%	26.0%	
2020	ARI	MLB	26	1.56	6.58	110	0.2	96.1	54.0%	24.9%	
2021 FS	ARI	MLB	27	1.25	3.73	90	2.2	96.0	54.7%	24.4%	47.9%
2021 DC	ARI	MLB	27	1.25	3.73	90	1.7	96.0	54.7%	24.4%	47.9%

Luke Weaver, continued

Pitch Shape vs LHH

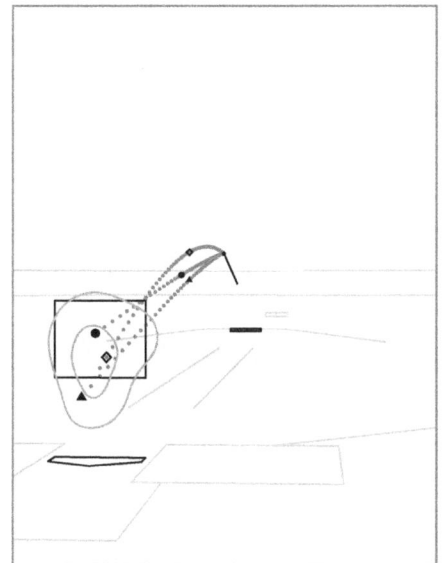

Pitch Shape vs RHH

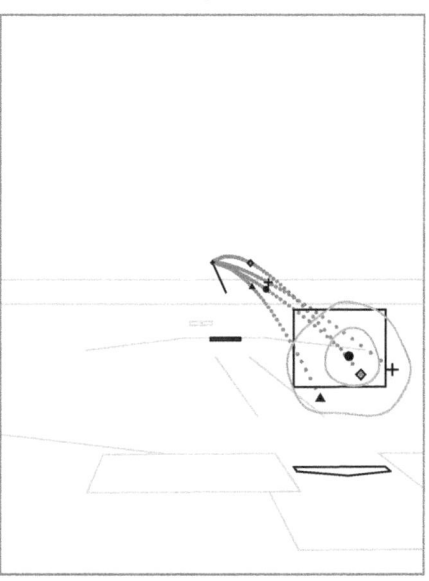

Type	Frequency	Velocity	H Movement	V Movement
● Fastball	54.0%	94 [104]	-6.7 [100]	-11.6 [110]
+ Cutter	11.8%	88.2 [99]	2.3 [103]	-21.4 [111]
▲ Changeup	27.3%	84.6 [98]	-12 [98]	-24.8 [107]
◇ Curveball	6.9%	78.9 [101]	3 [82]	-47.7 [101]

Taylor Widener RHP

Born: 10/24/94 Age: 26 Bats: L Throws: R
Height: 6'0" Weight: 230 Origin: Round 12, 2016 Draft (#368 overall)

YEAR	TEAM	LVL	AGE	W	L	SV	G	GS	IP	H	HR	BB/9	K/9	K	GB%	BABIP
2018	JXN	AA	23	5	8	0	26	25	137^1	99	12	2.8	11.5	176	34.8%	.276
2019	RNO	AAA	24	6	7	0	23	23	100	133	23	3.7	9.8	109	30.8%	.383
2020	ARI	MLB	25	0	1	0	12	0	20	14	5	5.4	9.9	22	37.3%	.196
2021 FS	ARI	MLB	26	2	2	0	57	0	50	45	8	4.2	9.7	53	34.2%	.289
2021 DC	ARI	MLB	26	2	2	0	51	0	46.7	42	7	4.2	9.7	50	34.2%	.289

Comparables: Nabil Crismatt, Tyler Thornburg, Ryan Helsley

Widener's debut season didn't exactly go as he'd hoped. His relative lack of height, mixed with a flat fastball and iffy command, made for some ugly outings. Once thought of as a rotation option, he'll need to turn things around in 2021 just to prove he belongs in the bullpen.

YEAR	TEAM	LVL	AGE	WHIP	ERA	DRA-	WARP	MPH	FB%	WHF	CSP
2018	JXN	AA	23	1.03	2.75	64	3.6				
2019	RNO	AAA	24	1.74	8.10	138	0.0				
2020	ARI	MLB	25	1.30	4.50	123	-0.1	96.2	65.1%	29.6%	
2021 FS	ARI	MLB	26	1.38	4.42	102	0.2	96.2	65.1%	29.6%	48.1%
2021 DC	ARI	MLB	26	1.38	4.42	102	0.2	96.2	65.1%	29.6%	48.1%

Taylor Widener, continued

Pitch Shape vs LHH

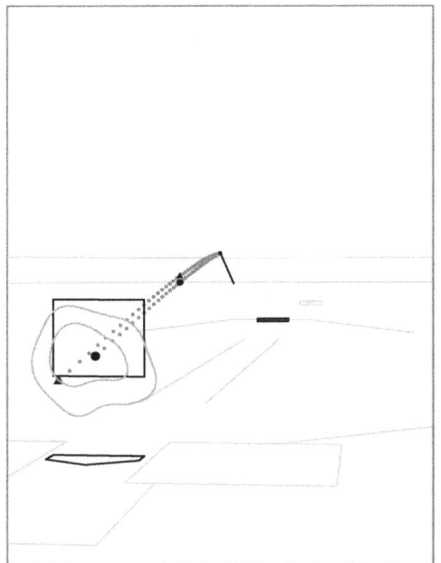

Pitch Shape vs RHH

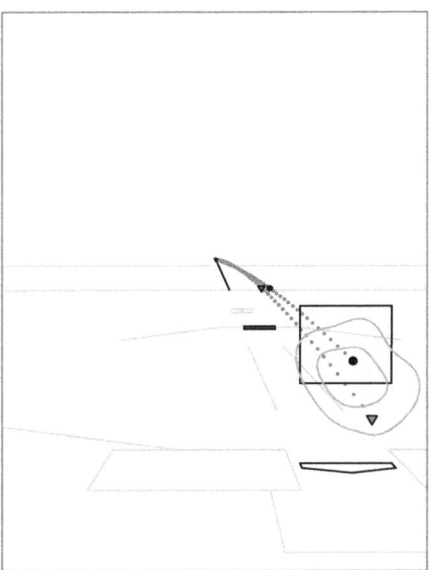

Type	Frequency	Velocity	H Movement	V Movement
● Fastball	64.6%	94.4 [106]	-6.2 [103]	-12.4 [108]
▲ Changeup	13.9%	86.2 [104]	-14.4 [86]	-26.6 [102]
▽ Slider	20.7%	85.8 [108]	5 [99]	-32.8 [103]

Alex Young LHP

Born: 09/09/93   Age: 27   Bats: L   Throws: L
Height: 6'3"   Weight: 220   Origin: Round 2, 2015 Draft (#43 overall)

YEAR	TEAM	LVL	AGE	W	L	SV	G	GS	IP	H	HR	BB/9	K/9	K	GB%	BABIP
2018	JXN	AA	24	5	1	0	9	9	50²	49	3	2.8	8.5	48	37.4%	.324
2018	RNO	AAA	24	5	4	0	20	12	80	99	12	2.6	6.9	61	42.4%	.341
2019	RNO	AAA	25	4	3	0	20	8	54²	66	6	4.3	10.5	64	48.8%	.380
2019	ARI	MLB	25	7	5	0	17	15	83¹	72	14	2.9	7.7	71	48.6%	.252
2020	ARI	MLB	26	2	4	0	15	7	46¹	51	11	2.7	7.6	39	36.7%	.288
2021 FS	ARI	MLB	27	9	8	0	26	26	150	145	22	3.3	8.1	134	41.8%	.288
2021 DC	ARI	MLB	27	6	4	0	52	6	57.7	56	8	3.3	8.1	51	41.8%	.288

Comparables: Matt Hall, Ryan Borucki, Max Fried

They say money isn't everything but it makes life a lot easier. It seems like one would need a pretty large sum to test that hypothesis, but the logic checks out. If velocity is currency for pitchers, Young got richer by adding a tick to his fastball and its sinking and cutting variants last year. That's no small deal for Young, a guy who was pushing toward the mid-90s at times in college but registered an average fastball velo below 90 mph in 2019 as a first-time big-leaguer. The problem is that he didn't get much for his money. His meager strikeout rate held as did his ability to limit walks, but what made him vulnerable is what happened when batters made contact. In that regard, he fared terribly and there's no simple remedy.

YEAR	TEAM	LVL	AGE	WHIP	ERA	DRA-	WARP	MPH	FB%	WHF	CSP
2018	JXN	AA	24	1.28	3.91	75	1.0				
2018	RNO	AAA	24	1.52	5.96	95	1.0				
2019	RNO	AAA	25	1.68	6.09	89	1.1				
2019	ARI	MLB	25	1.19	3.56	88	1.3	90.6	59.4%	27.4%	
2020	ARI	MLB	26	1.40	5.44	137	-0.5	92.2	54.6%	24.5%	
2021 FS	ARI	MLB	27	1.34	4.17	100	1.4	91.4	57.1%	26.0%	45.6%
2021 DC	ARI	MLB	27	1.34	4.17	100	0.5	91.4	57.1%	26.0%	45.6%

Alex Young, continued

Pitch Shape vs LHH

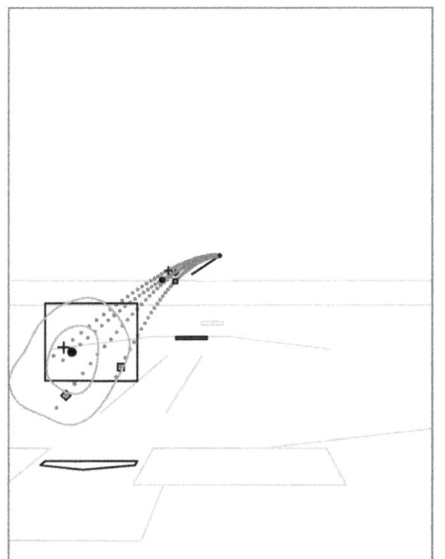

Pitch Shape vs RHH

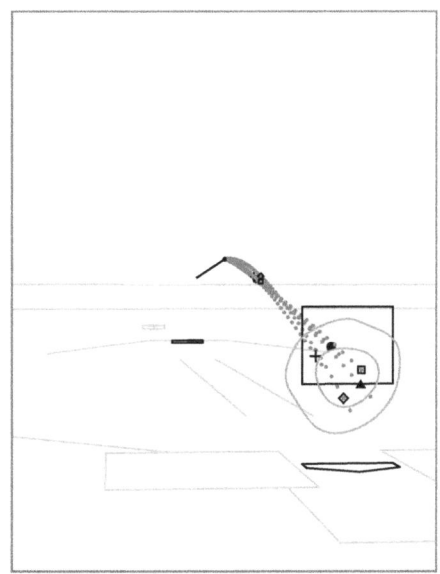

Type	Frequency	Velocity	H Movement	V Movement
● Fastball	18.9%	91.3 [96]	8.6 [91]	-15.5 [99]
☐ Sinker	13.9%	90.2 [89]	14.8 [87]	-22.4 [94]
+ Cutter	21.7%	86.6 [89]	0.1 [87]	-23.5 [103]
▲ Changeup	20.6%	85.1 [100]	12.8 [94]	-30.1 [93]
◇ Curveball	24.8%	81.6 [112]	-2.4 [79]	-38.7 [122]

PLAYER COMMENTS WITHOUT GRAPHS

Seth Beer LF
Born: 09/18/96   Age: 24   Bats: L   Throws: R
Height: 6'3"   Weight: 225   Origin: Round 1, 2018 Draft (#28 overall)

YEAR	TEAM	LVL	AGE	PA	R	2B	3B	HR	RBI	BB	K	SB	CS	AVG/OBP/SLG
2018	TRI	SS	21	51	9	3	0	4	7	6	10	0	0	.293/.431/.659
2018	QC	LO-A	21	132	15	7	0	3	16	15	17	1	0	.348/.443/.491
2018	FAY	HI-A	21	114	15	4	0	5	19	4	22	0	1	.262/.307/.439
2019	FAY	HI-A	22	152	24	8	0	9	34	14	30	0	3	.328/.414/.602
2019	CC	AA	22	280	40	9	0	16	52	24	58	0	0	.299/.407/.543
2019	JXN	AA	22	101	8	7	0	1	17	8	25	0	1	.205/.297/.318
2021 FS	ARI	MLB	24	600	70	25	3	23	77	44	159	0	0	.247/.327/.439

Comparables: Anthony Santander, Michael Taylor, Greg Bird

Chase Field has some issues. First and foremost, it lacks some charm even for those who frequent the stadium. The air conditioning runs at high capacity for much of the baseball season. The need to keep the roof closed for large swaths of the calendar makes it so difficult to grow grass that the team opts for artificial turf. Then there are matters of ownership and upkeep which result in legal battles aplenty. But Chase Field has one thing surely going for it: The beer prices are perennially amongst the lowest in the league. That counts for something, right? The Beer in question here has to be encouraged about the strong prospects of a DH in the National League because that's where he's best suited. He won't hit cheapies, either. If all goes according to plan, Beer may just raise the price of admission at Chase Field before long.

YEAR	TEAM	LVL	AGE	PA	DRC+	BABIP	BRR	FRAA	WARP
2018	TRI	SS	21	51	177	.296	-0.8	LF(7): -1.0, 1B(4): -0.1	0.1
2018	QC	LO-A	21	132	160	.391	-1.2	RF(10): -0.9, LF(9): -1.1, 1B(7): -0.5	0.6
2018	FAY	HI-A	21	114	106	.287	-2.2	LF(13): -1.4, 1B(6): -0.2	-0.4
2019	FAY	HI-A	22	152	188	.359	-1.6	1B(16): 0.0, LF(15): -0.7	1.3
2019	CC	AA	22	280	176	.333	-3.1	1B(46): 0.8, LF(8): -0.1	2.1
2019	JXN	AA	22	101	74	.270	0.0	1B(14): -0.7, LF(10): -0.4	-0.2
2021 FS	ARI	MLB	24	600	111	.308	-0.7	1B 0, LF 1	2.0

Corbin Carroll OF

Born: 08/21/00   Age: 20   Bats: L   Throws: L
Height: 5'10"   Weight: 165   Origin: Round 1, 2019 Draft (#16 overall)

YEAR	TEAM	LVL	AGE	PA	R	2B	3B	HR	RBI	BB	K	SB	CS	AVG/OBP/SLG
2019	DIA	ROK	18	137	23	6	3	2	14	24	29	16	1	.288/.409/.450
2019	HIL	SS	18	49	13	3	4	0	6	5	12	2	0	.326/.408/.581
2021 FS	ARI	MLB	20	600	45	21	7	7	49	45	203	21	4	.197/.262/.302

Comparables: Ronald Acuña Jr., Aaron Hicks, Trent Grisham

One doesn't have to look far ahead to see what's coming in the very near future. Carroll will be given every moniker, every descriptor, every platitude that Diamondbacks fans have heard applied to countless others over the years. He will run the bases like a man possessed, just like Eric Byrnes did. He will do the little things well, just like Chris Owings did. He will play with absolute grit and determination, just like Willie Bloomquist did. He will excel defensively just like Cliff Pennington did. These narratives have been alive and well in Arizona for some time and Carroll is going to have to get used to them. But there's one other thing—Carroll has talent more reminiscent of Justin Upton. Here's to hoping the Diamondbacks can work that into their spiel, too.

YEAR	TEAM	LVL	AGE	PA	DRC+	BABIP	BRR	FRAA	WARP
2019	DIA	ROK	18	137		.366			
2019	HIL	SS	18	49	116	.452	0.8	CF(11): 0.0	0.3
2021 FS	ARI	MLB	20	600	56	.297	2.6	CF 1, LF 0	-1.2

Arizona Diamondbacks 2021

Kevin Cron 1B
Born: 02/17/93 Age: 28 Bats: R Throws: R
Height: 6'5" Weight: 255 Origin: Round 14, 2014 Draft (#420 overall)

YEAR	TEAM	LVL	AGE	PA	R	2B	3B	HR	RBI	BB	K	SB	CS	AVG/OBP/SLG
2018	RNO	AAA	25	438	57	28	1	22	97	36	100	1	0	.309/.368/.554
2019	RNO	AAA	26	377	81	20	1	38	105	61	77	1	2	.331/.449/.777
2019	ARI	MLB	26	78	12	4	0	6	16	4	28	0	1	.211/.269/.521
2020	ARI	MLB	27	20	0	0	0	0	0	1	7	0	0	.000/.150/.000
2021 FS	ARI	MLB	28	600	76	24	1	32	89	49	195	0	1	.232/.305/.468

Comparables: Josh Whitesell, Tyler Moore, Mark Hamilton

While it may come as a surprise, there's a budding market for collectible VHS tapes. No kidding—those clunky tapes we all watched, complete with their poor sound quality and worse picture, have some market value these days. Nostalgia can get the best of us sometimes, and that's where Cron comes in. His big self has a big swing that can lead to big power when he squares up the baseball, but that doesn't happen very often. Cron is not a dynamic player and even with the DH in the National League this season he would look out of position. He would have been your prototypical masher a decade or two ago. But these days? Well, he's an outdated archetype in an evolved game that frankly requires more refinement than Cron has ever shown. He's about to find out if VHS tapes work any better in the NPB.

YEAR	TEAM	LVL	AGE	PA	DRC+	BABIP	BRR	FRAA	WARP
2018	RNO	AAA	25	438	125	.359	0.0	3B(57): -3.7, 1B(46): 6.6	2.2
2019	RNO	AAA	26	377	178	.328	-2.3	1B(69): 8.2, 3B(15): -0.3	4.5
2019	ARI	MLB	26	78	83	.237	-0.1	1B(12): -0.4, 3B(1): -0.0	0.0
2020	ARI	MLB	27	20	75	.000		1B(1): -0.0	0.0
2021 FS	ARI	MLB	28	600	110	.293	-0.9	1B 2, 3B -1	1.7

Jon Jay OF

Born: 03/15/85   Age: 36   Bats: L   Throws: L
Height: 5'11"   Weight: 200   Origin: Round 2, 2006 Draft (#74 overall)

YEAR	TEAM	LVL	AGE	PA	R	2B	3B	HR	RBI	BB	K	SB	CS	AVG/OBP/SLG
2018	KC	MLB	33	266	28	9	2	1	18	19	39	3	2	.307/.363/.374
2018	ARI	MLB	33	320	46	10	5	2	22	14	56	1	1	.235/.304/.325
2019	CHA	AAA	34	55	8	2	0	0	6	2	10	1	0	.358/.382/.396
2019	CHW	MLB	34	182	12	8	0	0	9	8	30	0	0	.267/.311/.315
2020	ARI	MLB	35	57	5	1	0	1	4	3	12	0	0	.160/.211/.240
2021 FS	ARI	MLB	36	600	52	22	3	6	50	38	129	5	2	.241/.312/.330

Comparables: Marquis Grissom, Coco Crisp, Mike Devereaux

Jay's second tour of duty with the Diamondbacks was a brief one. The shortened season cut into his opportunities, but not as much as his poor performance did.

YEAR	TEAM	LVL	AGE	PA	DRC+	BABIP	BRR	FRAA	WARP
2018	KC	MLB	33	266	79	.360	-0.5	LF(27): 1.2, CF(15): 1.8, RF(9): 0.2	0.3
2018	ARI	MLB	33	320	80	.284	-0.1	RF(45): 1.9, LF(14): -1.9, CF(10): -0.5	-0.1
2019	CHA	AAA	34	55	93	.442	0.0	RF(11): -1.4	-0.1
2019	CHW	MLB	34	182	77	.324	0.3	RF(33): -4.6, LF(13): -1.6	-0.7
2020	ARI	MLB	35	57	87	.175	0.0	RF(9): 0.4, CF(5): 0.1, LF(4): -0.1	0.0
2021 FS	ARI	MLB	36	600	79	.307	0.0	RF 2, LF 0	0.1

Arizona Diamondbacks 2021

Adam Jones RF
Born: 08/01/85   Age: 35   Bats: R   Throws: R
Height: 6'2"   Weight: 215   Origin: Round 1, 2003 Draft (#37 overall)

YEAR	TEAM	LVL	AGE	PA	R	2B	3B	HR	RBI	BB	K	SB	CS	AVG/OBP/SLG
2018	BAL	MLB	32	613	54	35	0	15	63	24	93	7	1	.281/.313/.419
2019	ARI	MLB	33	528	66	25	1	16	67	31	101	2	1	.260/.313/.414
2020	ORX	NPB	34	338	29	12	0	12	43	32	66	1	0	.258/.331/.417
2021 FS	ARI	MLB	35	600	59	25	1	16	66	30	128	2	2	.251/.298/.391

Comparables: Torii Hunter, Dave Henderson, Roberto Kelly

Jones's first foray in the NPB might have seemed disappointing to Buffaloes fans who expected more from the five-time MLB All-Star. In the meantime, he was dealing with everything, from a new country and culture to a language barrier and, most notably, an unusual schedule. While nagging minor injuries forced him to miss 37 games, he did show flashes of his talent when in the lineup, launching moonshots to the fifth deck at Osaka Dome in addition to notching the 2,000th base hit of his career between MLB and NPB on September 10. Considering his age, he might just be a league-average hitter in the NPB at this point, which would still be a major upgrade over what Orix could otherwise offer in 2021. That may be a bit of a letdown for those nostalgic for the days of yore, when stars like Reggie Smith and Bob Horner cast their limelight on the league, but it's pretty easily one of the lesser letdowns of the year.

YEAR	TEAM	LVL	AGE	PA	DRC+	BABIP	BRR	FRAA	WARP
2018	BAL	MLB	32	613	99	.311	1.0	CF(106): -11.8, RF(33): 2.0, LF(2): 0.1	1.0
2019	ARI	MLB	33	528	90	.296	1.0	RF(130): -6.2, CF(1): -0.0	0.1
2020	ORX	NPB	34	338					
2021 FS	ARI	MLB	35	600	89	.297	-0.6	RF 0, CF -4	0.1

Domingo Leyba 2B
Born: 09/11/95   Age: 25   Bats: S   Throws: R
Height: 5'11"   Weight: 200   Origin: International Free Agent, 2006

YEAR	TEAM	LVL	AGE	PA	R	2B	3B	HR	RBI	BB	K	SB	CS	AVG/OBP/SLG
2018	JXN	AA	22	358	43	17	2	5	30	35	46	5	2	.269/.344/.381
2019	RNO	AAA	23	498	85	37	3	19	77	32	78	0	2	.300/.351/.519
2019	ARI	MLB	23	30	6	2	1	0	5	4	9	0	0	.280/.367/.440
2021 FS	ARI	MLB	25	600	58	25	3	15	63	44	130	0	1	.239/.300/.380

Comparables: Brent Lillibridge, Stephen Drew, Matt Reynolds

Domingo Leyba didn't see any action in 2020 due to a preseason suspension for performance-enhancing drug Boldenone. Beyond that, injuries have robbed Leyba of critical development time over three of the past four seasons.

YEAR	TEAM	LVL	AGE	PA	DRC+	BABIP	BRR	FRAA	WARP
2018	JXN	AA	22	358	113	.300	-1.7	2B(72): -2.9, SS(8): 0.5	0.5
2019	RNO	AAA	23	498	92	.325	2.9	SS(67): -4.0, 2B(42): 2.9, 3B(2): 0.0	1.7
2019	ARI	MLB	23	30	84	.412	0.0	2B(8): 0.4, SS(2): 0.1, 3B(1): -0.0	0.1
2021 FS	ARI	MLB	25	600	88	.287	-0.6	2B 1, SS -1	0.8

Wyatt Mathisen 3B

Born: 12/30/93 Age: 27 Bats: R Throws: R
Height: 6'0" Weight: 210 Origin: Round 2, 2012 Draft (#69 overall)

YEAR	TEAM	LVL	AGE	PA	R	2B	3B	HR	RBI	BB	K	SB	CS	AVG/OBP/SLG
2018	ALT	AA	24	41	9	3	1	1	3	11	7	1	1	.385/.585/.692
2018	IND	AAA	24	282	34	13	0	9	45	23	59	2	2	.248/.330/.413
2019	DIA	ROK	25	31	4	3	0	0	3	6	3	1	0	.348/.516/.478
2019	RNO	AAA	25	345	72	19	1	23	61	39	84	1	0	.283/.403/.601
2020	ARI	MLB	26	33	5	0	0	2	5	5	12	0	0	.222/.364/.444
2021 FS	ARI	MLB	27	600	76	22	2	22	75	56	167	0	1	.231/.323/.411
2021 DC	ARI	MLB	27	95	12	3	0	3	11	9	26	0	0	.231/.323/.411

Comparables: Jefry Marte, Mike Brosseau, Matthew Brown

The 69th-overall pick in the 2012 draft, Mathisen slid nicely into his big-league debut in 2020. He's the kind of Quad-A player that teams covet as he can handle a few infield spots, though he's best at the corners, and has finally figured out how to tap into his power more regularly.

YEAR	TEAM	LVL	AGE	PA	DRC+	BABIP	BRR	FRAA	WARP
2018	ALT	AA	24	41	193	.474	-0.2	1B(5): -0.3, 2B(5): 0.7, 3B(1): 0.1	0.5
2018	IND	AAA	24	282	115	.285	1.2	1B(57): -0.0, 3B(15): -2.1, 2B(1): -0.1	0.5
2019	DIA	ROK	25	31		.400			
2019	RNO	AAA	25	345	122	.318	0.1	3B(59): 0.2, 2B(20): 0.6, 1B(9): 0.1	2.2
2020	ARI	MLB	26	33	97	.308	0.1	3B(7): 0.2	0.1
2021 FS	ARI	MLB	27	600	104	.293	-0.7	3B -2, 1B 0	1.2
2021 DC	ARI	MLB	27	95	104	.293	-0.1	3B 0	0.2

Arizona Diamondbacks 2021

Geraldo Perdomo SS

Born: 10/22/99   Age: 21   Bats: S   Throws: R
Height: 6'2"   Weight: 185   Origin: International Free Agent, 2016

YEAR	TEAM	LVL	AGE	PA	R	2B	3B	HR	RBI	BB	K	SB	CS	AVG/OBP/SLG
2018	DIA	ROK	18	101	20	4	2	1	8	14	17	14	1	.314/.416/.442
2018	MIS	ROK	18	29	3	0	1	0	2	7	4	1	1	.455/.586/.545
2018	HIL	SS	18	127	20	3	2	3	14	18	23	9	4	.301/.421/.456
2019	KC	LO-A	19	385	48	16	3	2	36	56	56	20	8	.268/.394/.357
2019	VIS	HI-A	19	114	15	5	0	1	11	14	11	6	5	.301/.407/.387
2021 FS	ARI	MLB	21	600	65	22	4	7	55	57	148	15	9	.231/.313/.335
2021 DC	ARI	MLB	21	33	3	1	0	0	3	3	8	0	1	.231/.313/.335

Comparables: J.P. Crawford, Asdrúbal Cabrera, Hanser Alberto

    Choose your own adventure books were all the rage in the '90s. Perdomo wouldn't know much about them, having been born in October of '99. That hasn't stopped him from striking out on his own path, though he isn't much for striking out otherwise. The lanky shortstop has supreme control of the strike zone for someone so young, and the big question with his bat is whether he'll fill out his frame enough to develop game power. His slick up-the-middle glove paired with a precocious approach should propel him to the majors, so whatever adventure he chooses, it'll have a major-league backdrop.

YEAR	TEAM	LVL	AGE	PA	DRC+	BABIP	BRR	FRAA	WARP
2018	DIA	ROK	18	101		.382			
2018	MIS	ROK	18	29		.556			
2018	HIL	SS	18	127	148	.359	1.4	SS(30): 3.9	1.3
2019	KC	LO-A	19	385	126	.318	-2.2	SS(80): 2.1, 2B(11): -0.1	2.7
2019	VIS	HI-A	19	114	128	.325	-0.2	SS(26): -1.0	0.6
2021 FS	ARI	MLB	21	600	83	.305	1.5	SS 1, 2B 0	0.8
2021 DC	ARI	MLB	21	33	83	.305	0.1	SS 0	0.0

Kristian Robinson CF

Born: 12/11/00 Age: 20 Bats: R Throws: R
Height: 6'3" Weight: 190 Origin: International Free Agent, 2017

YEAR	TEAM	LVL	AGE	PA	R	2B	3B	HR	RBI	BB	K	SB	CS	AVG/OBP/SLG
2018	DIA	ROK	17	182	35	11	0	4	31	16	46	7	5	.272/.341/.414
2018	MIS	ROK	17	74	13	1	0	3	10	11	21	5	3	.300/.419/.467
2019	HIL	SS	18	189	29	10	1	9	35	23	47	14	3	.319/.407/.558
2019	KC	LO-A	18	102	14	3	1	5	16	8	29	3	2	.217/.294/.435
2021 FS	ARI	MLB	20	600	50	20	2	12	54	40	222	13	7	.195/.256/.310

Comparables: Yorman Rodriguez, Domingo Santana, Nomar Mazara

Is it too early to dub Robinson the Bahamian Beast? Okay, maybe the moniker is a scoche premature, but the writing is on the wall. Players of his size with his level of athleticism don't grow on trees and there are simply things that Robinson can do that others can't. He turned heads at the Diamondbacks' alternate site all summer long and, according to reports, really grew as a ballplayer. His acumen for the game developed rapidly as he saw much more advanced pitching than ever before. In short, he's figuring it out and doing so quickly. For all he can do that others can't, though, he's going to have to prove he can consistently make contact before he truly makes the leap.

YEAR	TEAM	LVL	AGE	PA	DRC+	BABIP	BRR	FRAA	WARP
2018	DIA	ROK	17	182		.351			
2018	MIS	ROK	17	74		.405			
2019	HIL	SS	18	189	208	.398	-0.1	CF(22): 1.6, RF(18): 3.8	2.8
2019	KC	LO-A	18	102	90	.259	-0.3	CF(18): 0.6, RF(5): 0.2, LF(2): -0.3	0.2
2021 FS	ARI	MLB	20	600	55	.300	1.3	CF 5, RF 3	-0.8

Arizona Diamondbacks 2021

Pavin Smith 1B
Born: 02/06/96   Age: 25   Bats: L   Throws: L
Height: 6'2"   Weight: 210   Origin: Round 1, 2017 Draft (#7 overall)

YEAR	TEAM	LVL	AGE	PA	R	2B	3B	HR	RBI	BB	K	SB	CS	AVG/OBP/SLG
2018	VIS	HI-A	22	504	63	25	1	11	54	57	65	3	2	.255/.343/.392
2019	JXN	AA	23	507	62	29	6	12	67	59	61	2	1	.291/.370/.466
2020	ARI	MLB	24	44	7	0	1	1	4	5	8	1	0	.270/.341/.405
2021 FS	ARI	MLB	25	600	73	27	7	14	68	56	114	0	1	.252/.327/.411
2021 DC	ARI	MLB	25	350	42	15	4	8	40	33	66	0	0	.252/.327/.411

Comparables: Rangel Ravelo, Jordan Brown, Chris Parmelee

There's no denying that the lumbering slugger has really faded in popularity across baseball. The optimization of swings has resulted in smaller, slighter players being able to hit the ball hard enough— and far enough—to warrant regular playing time while their teams accumulate the benefits associated with greater athleticism. Smith certainly has the latter—he's quite athletic for a first baseman and can even play left field in a pinch. But the former prerequisite—that whole optimized swing thing—still seems to evade him dating back to his days at the University of Virginia. His 2020 big-league debut was fine aside from the continued absence of power production. If he can find his way to in-game power, he'll be one of the more well-rounded cold cornermen in the game.

YEAR	TEAM	LVL	AGE	PA	DRC+	BABIP	BRR	FRAA	WARP
2018	VIS	HI-A	22	504	112	.275	-1.1	1B(109): 9.0, RF(1): -0.1	0.6
2019	JXN	AA	23	507	142	.310	-5.9	1B(79): 2.5, RF(28): -2.6, LF(13): 1.0	2.5
2020	ARI	MLB	24	44	90	.300	-0.2	1B(5): 0.2, LF(3): 0.1, RF(2): -0.3	-0.1
2021 FS	ARI	MLB	25	600	100	.297	0.0	1B 1, RF 0	1.0
2021 DC	ARI	MLB	25	350	100	.297	0.0	1B 1, RF 0	0.6

Alek Thomas CF
Born: 04/28/00   Age: 21   Bats: L   Throws: L
Height: 5'11"   Weight: 175   Origin: Round 2, 2018 Draft (#63 overall)

YEAR	TEAM	LVL	AGE	PA	R	2B	3B	HR	RBI	BB	K	SB	CS	AVG/OBP/SLG
2018	MIS	ROK	18	134	26	11	1	2	17	11	19	4	3	.341/.396/.496
2018	DIA	ROK	18	138	24	3	5	0	10	13	18	8	2	.325/.394/.431
2019	KC	LO-A	19	402	63	21	7	8	48	43	72	11	6	.312/.393/.479
2019	VIS	HI-A	19	104	13	2	0	2	7	9	33	4	5	.255/.327/.340
2021 FS	ARI	MLB	21	600	52	24	6	10	57	36	163	6	6	.238/.289/.361

Comparables: Kyle Tucker, Albert Almora Jr., Manuel Margot

Let's take you back to your SAT days, but the ones before they added a writing section. We had it so easy, we just didn't know it.

Thomas : hitting :: DJ Khaled : winning.

We'll give you the answer: It's all either does, no matter what. It's as easy to overlook Thomas in the Diamondbacks center field picture as it is to ignore Khaled in a song that features Ludacris, Rick Ross, T-Pain, and Snoop Dogg, but do so at your own peril. Kristian Robinson and Corbin Carroll might garner most of the attention, but keep your eye on Thomas. He owns a gorgeous left-handed swing and plus raw power, and is advanced on both sides of the ball. Like Khaled, Thomas is also a grinder, and he receives rave reviews for his makeup and dedication to the game. One area they differ? Thomas is substance over flash, while the same can't be said for Khaled, though both will remind you of the value of putting in that work.

YEAR	TEAM	LVL	AGE	PA	DRC+	BABIP	BRR	FRAA	WARP
2018	MIS	ROK	18	134		.392			
2018	DIA	ROK	18	138		.381			
2019	KC	LO-A	19	402	153	.372	0.4	CF(76): -10.1, LF(7): 0.2, RF(7): 0.8	2.5
2019	VIS	HI-A	19	104	89	.373	0.4	CF(23): 2.6	0.6
2021 FS	ARI	MLB	21	600	76	.318	0.9	CF 1, LF 1	0.3

Josh VanMeter   LF
Born: 03/10/95   Age: 26   Bats: L   Throws: R
Height: 5'11"   Weight: 190   Origin: Round 5, 2013 Draft (#148 overall)

YEAR	TEAM	LVL	AGE	PA	R	2B	3B	HR	RBI	BB	K	SB	CS	AVG/OBP/SLG
2018	PNS	AA	23	121	13	10	0	1	14	23	19	5	2	.284/.420/.421
2018	LOU	AAA	23	362	40	25	6	11	45	28	73	5	3	.253/.309/.464
2019	LOU	AAA	24	211	43	14	1	14	43	24	37	8	3	.348/.429/.669
2019	CIN	MLB	24	260	33	13	1	8	23	29	56	9	3	.237/.327/.408
2020	CIN	MLB	25	38	3	1	0	1	3	1	16	1	0	.059/.158/.176
2020	ARI	MLB	25	41	6	2	0	1	5	4	8	0	0	.194/.293/.333
2021 FS	ARI	MLB	26	600	73	28	4	18	68	56	154	5	2	.228/.304/.401
2021 DC	ARI	MLB	26	103	12	4	0	3	11	9	26	0	1	.228/.304/.401

Comparables: Alex Gordon, Larry Bigbie, Ryan Langerhans

Every coin has two sides. Take, for example, 1870's French five-franc piece. On the first side is the goddess Ceres, a representative of agriculture, crops, and fertility. Ceres was a motherly figure above all else, and being a mother to the Third Republic is something you can hang your hat on. The reverse side denotes the coin's date and displays lush wreaths, a sign of freedom and prosperity. If VanMeter were a coin he'd have two distinct sides, too. One would be of a useful, athletic utility man in the Kiké Hernández mold. The other would be of a guy who just can't quite do enough with the stick to, well, stick. The Diamondbacks appear willing to flip that coin in 2021.

Arizona Diamondbacks 2021

YEAR	TEAM	LVL	AGE	PA	DRC+	BABIP	BRR	FRAA	WARP
2018	PNS	AA	23	121	145	.342	-0.4	LF(15): -0.9, 2B(9): -0.4, SS(5): -0.5	0.4
2018	LOU	AAA	23	362	109	.292	-2.7	2B(47): -3.8, LF(23): -1.3, 3B(10): 1.1	0.2
2019	LOU	AAA	24	211	159	.371	0.2	2B(22): 0.1, 1B(13): 0.4, 3B(10): -0.4	2.0
2019	CIN	MLB	24	260	99	.279	-1.2	LF(47): 2.3, 2B(18): 0.2, 1B(17): 0.4	0.8
2020	CIN	MLB	25	38	70	.059	0.3	2B(7): -0.2, 1B(3): -0.0	-0.1
2020	ARI	MLB	25	41	70	.222	-0.1	2B(10): -1.2, 3B(2): -0.0	-0.1
2021 FS	ARI	MLB	26	600	92	.284	0.1	2B -1, 3B 0	0.8
2021 DC	ARI	MLB	26	103	92	.284	0.0	2B 0, 3B 0	0.1

Stephen Vogt   C

Born: 11/01/84   Age: 36   Bats: L   Throws: R
Height: 6'0"   Weight: 211   Origin: Round 12, 2007 Draft (#365 overall)

YEAR	TEAM	LVL	AGE	PA	R	2B	3B	HR	RBI	BB	K	SB	CS	AVG/OBP/SLG
2019	SAC	AAA	34	72	9	3	0	4	7	14	11	0	0	.241/.389/.500
2019	SF	MLB	34	280	30	24	2	10	40	20	66	3	1	.263/.314/.490
2020	ARI	MLB	35	81	6	5	0	1	7	8	18	0	0	.167/.247/.278
2021 FS	ARI	MLB	36	600	67	25	3	16	69	52	140	2	1	.215/.288/.369
2021 DC	ARI	MLB	36	230	25	9	1	6	26	20	53	0	1	.215/.288/.369

Comparables: Lance Parrish, Mike Macfarlane, Javy Lopez

YEAR	TEAM	P. COUNT	FRM RUNS	BLK RUNS	THRW RUNS	TOT RUNS
2019	SF	7706	-1.6	-0.6	-0.5	-2.7
2020	ARI	2961	1.3	0.1	0.0	1.3
2021	ARI	8418	-1.6	0.2	0.2	-1.2
2021	ARI	8418	-1.6	1.0	0.2	-0.4

There's no real way to skirt around the fact that Vogt was quite bad last year. Yeah, it was a weird season, and yeah, Vogt was donning a new jersey, but nothing seemed to go right for the veteran. Brought in to serve as a sort of limited platoon partner with Carson Kelly, the lefty didn't hit righties well. The sample was tiny and perhaps that should limit any conclusions, but Vogt did a few things in particular that dragged down his BABIP and the rest of his line. He hit more ground balls, he hit them weakly, and he pulled them a bunch. That makes for some easy groundouts considering his (in)ability to run. Reversing course is paramount in 2021 considering his age and proximity to retirement.

YEAR	TEAM	LVL	AGE	PA	DRC+	BABIP	BRR	FRAA	WARP
2019	SAC	AAA	34	72	121	.233	-0.7	C(9): -0.3, 1B(6): -0.4, LF(1): -0.1	0.3
2019	SF	MLB	34	280	105	.311	-0.2	C(60): -1.0, LF(7): -0.2, 1B(1): 0.0	1.4
2020	ARI	MLB	35	81	88	.204	-0.5	C(23): -0.4, 1B(1): 0.1	0.2
2021 FS	ARI	MLB	36	600	80	.259	-0.2	C -1, 1B 0	0.6
2021 DC	ARI	MLB	36	230	80	.259	-0.1	C -1	0.3

Andy Young 2B

Born: 05/10/94   Age: 27   Bats: R   Throws: R
Height: 6'0"   Weight: 200   Origin: Round 37, 2016 Draft (#1126 overall)

YEAR	TEAM	LVL	AGE	PA	R	2B	3B	HR	RBI	BB	K	SB	CS	AVG/OBP/SLG
2018	PMB	HI-A	24	351	43	10	2	12	34	31	59	4	0	.276/.372/.444
2018	SPR	AA	24	152	18	3	1	9	24	7	26	0	2	.319/.395/.556
2019	JXN	AA	25	263	36	15	2	8	28	18	53	1	1	.260/.363/.453
2019	RNO	AAA	25	277	53	10	3	21	53	24	68	2	2	.280/.373/.611
2020	ARI	MLB	26	34	3	2	0	1	4	5	10	0	0	.192/.382/.385
2021 FS	ARI	MLB	27	600	82	21	5	26	79	41	174	0	1	.243/.327/.452
2021 DC	ARI	MLB	27	63	8	2	0	2	8	4	18	0	0	.243/.327/.452

Comparables: Josh Satin, Michael Hollimon, Drew Sutton

There's been plenty of dialogue over the last half decade regarding the trouble that modern baseball has caused for certain types of players. No longer can teams effectively hide terrible defenders in left field to make way for their bats. Most teams have chosen defensive value at catcher over an ability to hit. Starting pitchers just aren't used like workhorses anymore (with a few obvious exceptions). But some players benefit from the construction of the modern baseball roster and Young may be one of them. He doesn't have a true defensive home to speak of, but he can man a few spots serviceably, and the bat, well, that's the ticket. He can hit, has some pop, and can afford manager Torey Lovullo some luxuries in how he's deployed. He's unlikely to be an everyday guy, but instead a bench piece that gets steady action—a valuable player by today's standards.

YEAR	TEAM	LVL	AGE	PA	DRC+	BABIP	BRR	FRAA	WARP
2018	PMB	HI-A	24	351	137	.304	-0.1	2B(73): -4.5, 3B(7): -0.5, SS(1): -0.0	1.1
2018	SPR	AA	24	152	146	.340	-0.9	2B(30): -2.8, 3B(7): -0.7	0.4
2019	JXN	AA	25	263	128	.305	-0.3	2B(47): -2.5, SS(8): -1.1, 3B(6): 0.2	1.2
2019	RNO	AAA	25	277	109	.305	0.9	SS(25): 1.3, 3B(23): -1.0, 2B(22): 0.1	1.5
2020	ARI	MLB	26	34	96	.267	0.0	2B(4): -0.1, 3B(3): -0.5, LF(1): -0.0	0.0
2021 FS	ARI	MLB	27	600	116	.308	-0.1	SS -1, 2B 0	2.8
2021 DC	ARI	MLB	27	63	116	.308	0.0	SS 0	0.3

Arizona Diamondbacks 2021

Jeremy Beasley RHP
Born: 11/20/95   Age: 25   Bats: R   Throws: R
Height: 6'3"   Weight: 245   Origin: Round 30, 2017 Draft (#895 overall)

YEAR	TEAM	LVL	AGE	W	L	SV	G	GS	IP	H	HR	BB/9	K/9	K	GB%	BABIP
2018	BUR	LO-A	22	0	2	0	6	5	23	16	0	2.7	7.4	19	39.7%	.254
2018	IE	HI-A	22	3	2	1	9	6	44¹	48	4	2.2	9.7	48	40.9%	.364
2018	MOB	AA	22	3	3	0	10	7	44¹	32	3	2.8	7.5	37	41.7%	.248
2019	MOB	AA	23	6	7	0	23	22	108²	110	13	3.5	8.4	102	46.2%	.312
2019	SL	AAA	23	1	0	0	3	3	13²	19	1	4.0	8.6	13	37.0%	.400
2020	ARI	MLB	24	0	0	0	1	0	0¹	2	0	0.0	27.0	1	0.0%	1.000
2021 FS	ARI	MLB	25	2	3	0	57	0	50	48	7	4.2	8.1	44	41.8%	.288
2021 DC	ARI	MLB	25	0	0	0	3	3	12.7	12	1	4.2	8.1	11	41.8%	.288

Comparables: Robert Dugger, Jorge Alcala, P.J. Walters

If timing is everything then Beasley should ask for his money back. The righty acquired for Matt Andriese made one appearance, faced three batters, got one out, and suffered a shoulder injury that ended his season in 2020. He's either a back-end starter or a middle/long reliever long term, just like Andriese was.

YEAR	TEAM	LVL	AGE	WHIP	ERA	DRA-	WARP	MPH	FB%	WHF	CSP
2018	BUR	LO-A	22	1.00	2.35	79	0.4				
2018	IE	HI-A	22	1.33	3.05	93	0.3				
2018	MOB	AA	22	1.04	2.44	97	0.3				
2019	MOB	AA	23	1.40	4.06	106	-0.3				
2019	SL	AAA	23	1.83	7.90	121	0.1				
2020	ARI	MLB	24	6.00	0.00	78	0.0	92.4	37.5%	28.6%	
2021 FS	ARI	MLB	25	1.43	4.54	105	0.1	92.4	37.5%	28.6%	41.9%
2021 DC	ARI	MLB	25	1.43	4.54	105	0.0	92.4	37.5%	28.6%	41.9%

J.B. Bukauskas RHP
Born: 10/11/96   Age: 24   Bats: R   Throws: R
Height: 6'0"   Weight: 210   Origin: Round 1, 2017 Draft (#15 overall)

YEAR	TEAM	LVL	AGE	W	L	SV	G	GS	IP	H	HR	BB/9	K/9	K	GB%	BABIP
2018	AST	ROK	21	0	0	0	1	1	1²	5	0	0.0	10.8	2	12.5%	.625
2018	TRI	SS	21	0	0	0	3	3	8¹	8	0	2.2	9.7	9	45.5%	.364
2018	QC	LO-A	21	1	2	0	4	4	15	15	0	4.2	12.6	21	50.0%	.405
2018	FAY	HI-A	21	3	0	0	5	5	28	13	1	4.2	10.0	31	58.7%	.194
2018	CC	AA	21	0	0	0	1	1	6	1	0	3.0	12.0	8	60.0%	.100
2019	JXN	AA	22	0	1	0	2	2	7	10	0	6.4	14.1	11	38.9%	.556
2019	CC	AA	22	2	4	1	20	14	85²	81	8	5.7	10.3	98	46.1%	.332
2021 FS	ARI	MLB	24	2	3	0	57	0	50	44	6	6.0	9.4	52	43.4%	.284
2021 DC	ARI	MLB	24	4	3	0	31	6	45.7	40	6	6.0	9.4	48	43.4%	.284

Comparables: Carson Fulmer, Duane Underwood Jr., Jorge Alcala

Bukauskas continues to soldier on with an undefined role. The longer the decision takes, the more inevitable it seems that he'll become a reliever. That's okay because he has the tools to be a good one quite soon. Excellent relievers can be more valuable than fringy starters these days anyway.

YEAR	TEAM	LVL	AGE	WHIP	ERA	DRA-	WARP	MPH	FB%	WHF	CSP
2018	AST	ROK	21	3.00	10.80						
2018	TRI	SS	21	1.20	0.00	235	-0.5				
2018	QC	LO-A	21	1.47	4.20	33	0.6				
2018	FAY	HI-A	21	0.93	1.61	67	0.7				
2018	CC	AA	21	0.50	0.00	64	0.1				
2019	JXN	AA	22	2.14	7.71	150	-0.2				
2019	CC	AA	22	1.58	5.25	125	-1.3				
2021 FS	*ARI*	*MLB*	*24*	*1.55*	*4.74*	*108*	*0.0*				
2021 DC	*ARI*	*MLB*	*24*	*1.55*	*4.74*	*108*	*0.1*				

Slade Cecconi   RHP
Born: 06/24/99   Age: 22   Bats: R   Throws: R
Height: 6'4"   Weight: 219   Origin: Round 1, 2020 Draft (#33 overall)

Cecconi is short on track record but big on stuff. The 33rd-overall pick in June was a draft-eligible sophomore who can pump the gas. With a legit four-pitch mix and an ability to throw strikes, Cecconi has as much upside as any pitching prospect in the Diamondbacks' system, though he's yet to throw a professional pitch.

Chris Devenski   RHP
Born: 11/13/90   Age: 30   Bats: R   Throws: R
Height: 6'3"   Weight: 219   Origin: Round 25, 2011 Draft (#771 overall)

YEAR	TEAM	LVL	AGE	W	L	SV	G	GS	IP	H	HR	BB/9	K/9	K	GB%	BABIP
2018	HOU	MLB	27	2	3	2	50	1	47^1	42	9	2.5	9.7	51	33.3%	.277
2019	HOU	MLB	28	2	3	0	61	1	69	69	13	2.7	9.4	72	33.2%	.298
2020	HOU	MLB	29	0	1	0	4	0	3^2	7	1	7.4	12.3	5	46.2%	.500
2021 FS	*ARI*	*MLB*	*30*	*2*	*2*	*0*	*57*	*0*	*50*	*44*	*8*	*2.8*	*9.4*	*52*	*35.4%*	*.282*

Comparables: Ken Giles, Emilio Pagán, Hansel Robles

Devenski symbolized not only Houston's bullpen woes, but their struggles overall. A unit that was very recently one of the best in baseball fell apart, ravaged by injury and poor performance. His Astros tenure concluded with four appearances, two trips to the IL and season-ending surgery to remove a bone spur in his troublesome elbow.

Arizona Diamondbacks 2021

YEAR	TEAM	LVL	AGE	WHIP	ERA	DRA-	WARP	MPH	FB%	WHF	CSP
2018	HOU	MLB	27	1.16	4.18	80	0.7	95.9	41.6%	31.6%	
2019	HOU	MLB	28	1.30	4.83	112	-0.1	96.6	44.1%	28.2%	
2020	HOU	MLB	29	2.73	14.73	81	0.1	94.1	38.5%	30.0%	
2021 FS	ARI	MLB	30	1.20	3.61	84	0.7	96.3	43.0%	29.1%	46.1%

Jon Duplantier RHP
Born: 07/11/94   Age: 26   Bats: L   Throws: R
Height: 6'4"   Weight: 240   Origin: Round 3, 2016 Draft (#89 overall)

YEAR	TEAM	LVL	AGE	W	L	SV	G	GS	IP	H	HR	BB/9	K/9	K	GB%	BABIP
2018	DIA	ROK	23	0	0	0	2	2	7	5	0	2.6	11.6	9	43.8%	.312
2018	JXN	AA	23	5	1	0	14	14	67	52	4	3.8	9.1	68	54.0%	.284
2019	DIA	ROK	24	0	0	0	2	2	2	5	1	13.5	13.5	3	50.0%	.571
2019	VIS	HI-A	24	0	0	0	1	1	3	2	0	0.0	9.0	3	50.0%	.333
2019	RNO	AAA	24	1	2	0	13	11	38	31	1	6.6	10.4	44	44.7%	.330
2019	ARI	MLB	24	1	1	1	15	3	36²	39	2	4.4	8.3	34	42.5%	.359
2021 FS	ARI	MLB	26	2	3	0	57	0	50	46	6	4.8	9.3	51	45.4%	.297
2021 DC	ARI	MLB	26	3	2	0	28	3	33	30	4	4.8	9.3	34	45.4%	.297

Comparables: Ryan Helsley, Yonny Chirinos, Jordan Montgomery

Another year, another round of injuries for Duplantier. The former third-rounder was seen as a potential steal back in 2016, but the injury concerns that pushed him to the 89th overall pick have been a steady presence. It was elbow trouble in 2020 that kept the 26-year-old from contributing and he now seems destined for relief.

YEAR	TEAM	LVL	AGE	WHIP	ERA	DRA-	WARP	MPH	FB%	WHF	CSP
2018	DIA	ROK	23	1.00	1.29						
2018	JXN	AA	23	1.19	2.69	99	0.5				
2019	DIA	ROK	24	4.00	18.00						
2019	VIS	HI-A	24	0.67	0.00	103	0.0				
2019	RNO	AAA	24	1.55	5.21	60	1.4				
2019	ARI	MLB	24	1.55	4.42	117	-0.1	94.1	59.0%	20.6%	
2021 FS	ARI	MLB	26	1.46	4.61	105	0.1	94.1	59.0%	20.6%	47.9%
2021 DC	ARI	MLB	26	1.46	4.61	105	0.1	94.1	59.0%	20.6%	47.9%

Bryce Jarvis RHP
Born: 12/26/97   Age: 23   Bats: L   Throws: R
Height: 6'2"   Weight: 195   Origin: Round 1, 2020 Draft (#18 overall)

Not many people know that Duke University has a flux capacitor on campus. Fewer are aware that it is property of the baseball team. Jarvis was clearly the university's trial case because, as an underclassman, he was a total throwback. Upper-80s heater, good changeup, breaking balls that didn't vary in velo much from the fastball. After time traveling, Jarvis emerged his junior year as a guy who'd broken into the modern realm with a fastball approaching the mid 90s at times, and helping the rest of his arsenal play up. Strong, albeit abbreviated, results immediately followed, and Jarvis found himself selected in the middle of the first round of the 2020 draft. He could move quickly and is arguably the Diamondbacks' best pitching prospect.

Levi Kelly RHP
Born: 05/14/99   Age: 22   Bats: R   Throws: R
Height: 6'4"   Weight: 205   Origin: Round 8, 2018 Draft (#249 overall)

YEAR	TEAM	LVL	AGE	W	L	SV	G	GS	IP	H	HR	BB/9	K/9	K	GB%	BABIP
2018	DIA	ROK	19	0	0	0	4	4	6	3	0	3.0	9.0	6	46.7%	.200
2019	KC	LO-A	20	5	1	0	22	22	100^1	72	4	3.5	11.3	126	46.0%	.293
2021 FS	ARI	MLB	22	2	3	0	57	0	50	45	7	5.3	8.9	49	42.2%	.283

Comparables: Neftalí Feliz, Casey Crosby, Robert Stephenson

Adjusted expectations became the norm last year, and while all of the uncertainty threw some players off their game, Kelly took full advantage of the opportunity. The youngster made the Diamondbacks' 60-man roster, then proceeded to throw a handful of highly impressive relief innings in July against big-league regulars in summer camp, often making them look overmatched. In hindsight, striking out Eduardo Escobar looks less impressive now but Kelly flashed real, quality stuff. His mid-90s gas and deadly slider play right now, and his changeup flashes enough to give hope that he could have three quality offerings. The effort in his delivery still suggests a relief role, but look for the Diamondbacks to keep him as a starter a bit longer in hopes of turning the former eighth-round pick into a rotation piece.

YEAR	TEAM	LVL	AGE	WHIP	ERA	DRA-	WARP	MPH	FB%	WHF	CSP
2018	DIA	ROK	19	0.83	0.00						
2019	KC	LO-A	20	1.11	2.15	65	2.4				
2021 FS	ARI	MLB	22	1.50	4.85	110	0.0				

Arizona Diamondbacks 2021

Mike Leake RHP
Born: 11/12/87   Age: 33   Bats: R   Throws: R
Height: 5'10"   Weight: 165   Origin: Round 1, 2009 Draft (#8 overall)

YEAR	TEAM	LVL	AGE	W	L	SV	G	GS	IP	H	HR	BB/9	K/9	K	GB%	BABIP
2018	SEA	MLB	30	10	10	0	31	31	185²	207	23	1.6	5.8	119	49.4%	.307
2019	SEA	MLB	31	9	8	0	22	22	137	153	26	1.2	6.6	100	47.7%	.298
2019	ARI	MLB	31	3	3	0	10	10	60	74	15	1.2	4.0	27	45.0%	.292
2021 FS	ARI	MLB	33	9	9	0	26	26	150	162	24	1.9	6.5	108	46.8%	.296

Comparables: Jeremy Hellickson, Rick Porcello, Brad Radke

Leake was the first big-league player to opt out of the 2020 season. Now 33 years old, it remains to be seen if he can continue his durable, innings-eating, back-end starter ways.

YEAR	TEAM	LVL	AGE	WHIP	ERA	DRA-	WARP	MPH	FB%	WHF	CSP
2018	SEA	MLB	30	1.30	4.36	99	1.8	90.5	59.4%	16.8%	
2019	SEA	MLB	31	1.26	4.27	120	-0.2	90.1	58.9%	18.6%	
2019	ARI	MLB	31	1.37	4.35	184	-2.1	90.5	57.5%	17.1%	
2021 FS	ARI	MLB	33	1.30	4.40	106	0.9	90.4	58.8%	17.7%	50.9%

Corbin Martin RHP
Born: 12/28/95   Age: 25   Bats: R   Throws: R
Height: 6'2"   Weight: 228   Origin: Round 2, 2017 Draft (#56 overall)

YEAR	TEAM	LVL	AGE	W	L	SV	G	GS	IP	H	HR	BB/9	K/9	K	GB%	BABIP
2018	FAY	HI-A	22	2	0	1	4	3	19	4	0	3.3	12.3	26	63.9%	.111
2018	CC	AA	22	7	2	0	21	18	103	84	7	2.4	8.4	96	47.7%	.277
2019	RR	AAA	23	2	1	0	9	8	37¹	33	2	4.3	10.8	45	38.7%	.348
2019	HOU	MLB	23	1	1	0	5	5	19¹	23	8	5.6	8.8	19	42.6%	.283
2021 FS	ARI	MLB	25	9	8	0	26	26	150	133	21	4.2	9.3	155	42.1%	.284
2021 DC	ARI	MLB	25	1	1	0	8	6	25.7	23	3	4.2	9.3	26	42.1%	.284

Comparables: Brandon Bielak, Mitch Keller, Wade LeBlanc

Delayed gratification isn't something Americans are much accustomed to. Jeff Bezos and company have made acquiring tangible benefits easier than ever no matter where you live or what you seek. But there's something to be said for the buildup, for anticipation. When it comes to Martin, well, that's all the Diamondbacks can lean on. His recovery from Tommy John hasn't hit any publicly reported snags and it feels as if the best prospect acquired in the team's trade of Zack Greinke will finally see the field in Sedona Red come 2021. Considering Seth Beer's defensive issues and J.B. Bukauskas' strike-throwing troubles, a lot hinges on when, and more importantly, how Martin reacquaints himself with the majors.

YEAR	TEAM	LVL	AGE	WHIP	ERA	DRA-	WARP	MPH	FB%	WHF	CSP
2018	FAY	HI-A	22	0.58	0.00	65	0.5				
2018	CC	AA	22	1.09	2.97	69	2.3				
2019	RR	AAA	23	1.37	3.13	61	1.3				
2019	HOU	MLB	23	1.81	5.59	147	-0.3	97.2	62.6%	23.8%	
2021 FS	ARI	MLB	25	1.35	4.06	97	1.7	97.2	62.6%	23.8%	44.3%
2021 DC	ARI	MLB	25	1.35	4.06	97	0.3	97.2	62.6%	23.8%	44.3%

Keury Mella   RHP

Born: 08/02/93   Age: 27   Bats: R   Throws: R
Height: 6'2"   Weight: 230   Origin: International Free Agent, 2012

YEAR	TEAM	LVL	AGE	W	L	SV	G	GS	IP	H	HR	BB/9	K/9	K	GB%	BABIP
2018	PNS	AA	24	7	3	0	16	16	85	70	8	3.3	9.2	87	47.6%	.279
2018	LOU	AAA	24	2	1	0	5	5	23	20	1	2.3	5.5	14	39.4%	.275
2018	CIN	MLB	24	0	0	0	4	0	9^1	13	4	7.7	7.7	8	29.0%	.360
2019	LOU	AAA	25	8	14	0	27	27	142^2	160	22	3.5	6.4	102	52.0%	.308
2019	CIN	MLB	25	0	0	0	2	0	3^2	5	0	4.9	9.8	4	33.3%	.417
2020	ARI	MLB	26	2	0	0	11	0	10	10	1	2.7	9.0	10	44.8%	.321
2021 FS	ARI	MLB	27	2	3	0	57	0	50	48	7	4.0	7.7	42	45.9%	.286
2021 DC	ARI	MLB	27	2	3	0	57	0	53.3	51	7	4.0	7.7	45	45.9%	.286

Comparables: Chase De Jong, Drew Anderson, Lucas Sims

Early aughts alternative band Sum 41 had a hit on their hands with their album *All Killer, No Filler*. Mella fits that theme so long as one flips the title around. Don't let the ERA fool you—with his merely okay stuff and command, he can get in too deep and leave with a fat lip.

YEAR	TEAM	LVL	AGE	WHIP	ERA	DRA-	WARP	MPH	FB%	WHF	CSP
2018	PNS	AA	24	1.19	3.07	88	1.1				
2018	LOU	AAA	24	1.13	2.74	117	-0.1				
2018	CIN	MLB	24	2.25	8.68	201	-0.4	96.7	70.8%	24.1%	
2019	LOU	AAA	25	1.51	5.05	110	1.8				
2019	CIN	MLB	25	1.91	7.36	99	0.0	96.9	77.4%	27.8%	
2020	ARI	MLB	26	1.30	1.80	92	0.1	96.8	67.3%	24.3%	
2021 FS	ARI	MLB	27	1.42	4.60	106	0.1	96.8	69.1%	24.5%	46.6%
2021 DC	ARI	MLB	27	1.42	4.60	106	0.1	96.8	69.1%	24.5%	46.6%

Blake Walston LHP

Born: 06/28/01 Age: 20 Bats: L Throws: L
Height: 6'5" Weight: 175 Origin: Round 1, 2019 Draft (#26 overall)

YEAR	TEAM	LVL	AGE	W	L	SV	G	GS	IP	H	HR	BB/9	K/9	K	GB%	BABIP
2019	DIA	ROK	18	0	0	0	3	2	5	2	0	0.0	19.8	11	83.3%	.333
2019	HIL	SS	18	0	0	0	3	3	6	6	0	3.0	9.0	6	41.2%	.353
2021 FS	ARI	MLB	20	2	3	0	57	0	50	47	7	5.2	9.0	50	41.1%	.291

Comparables: Hunter Harvey, Jenrry Mejia, Noah Syndergaard

The saying is to never judge a book by its cover because it doesn't adequately relay to the reader what is going to happen in the book. The same can be true for pitching prospects, but sometimes what's on the surface is a good reflection of the whole package. So it is with Walston, who is the definition of "projectable" at a lean 6-foot-5. He'll sit in the low-to-mid 90s with his fastball, but the hope is he starts to see some velocity creep as he focuses on baseball (he was a quarterback in high school) and pack good weight onto his lanky frame. The curveball is a potential plus offering, but both his changeup and a recently developed slider lag behind. Add it all up and you get a mid-rotation outcome should everything come together, and more in the tank if there's a velocity bump. As with any book or prospect, though, you've got to read all the way to the end to know how it turns out.

YEAR	TEAM	LVL	AGE	WHIP	ERA	DRA-	WARP	MPH	FB%	WHF	CSP
2019	DIA	ROK	18	0.40	1.80						
2019	HIL	SS	18	1.33	3.00	122	-0.1				
2021 FS	ARI	MLB	20	1.52	5.04	116	-0.2				

Diamondbacks Prospects

The State of the System:
Another bumper crop of draft picks buoy an already-deep system, but the lost development year may affect the Diamondbacks org—or at least the variance and risk within—more than most.

The Top Ten:

─────── ★ ★ ★ *2021 Top 101 Prospect* **#15** ★ ★ ★ ───────

1 **Kristian Robinson** CF   OFP: 70   ETA: 2023
Born: 12/11/00   Age: 20   Bats: R   Throws: R   Height: 6'3"   Weight: 190
Origin: International Free Agent, 2017

The Report: We kick off our prospect lists with a teenager (at time of publication) who has one of the best power/speed combinations in the minors. The Baseball Prospectus Prospect Team is always on brand. Robinson is a plus runner with potential top-of-the-scale pop who has a good chance to be an above-average glove in center field. The other tools aren't as loud, but he potentially has all five; the hit tool is the thorniest, although that's not unusual given Robinson's limited pro experience. The swing-and-miss concerns do create a gap between the present and the projected and increase the out-and-out bust risk.

Development Track: There's an alternate history—hoo boy will this be a recurring theme in this section across all 30 lists—where Robinson torched both A-ball levels and established himself as one of the elite prospects in baseball. The tools are all there, and showed in enough flashes at the alternate site to more or less hold serve in the Top 101. Despite the lost year he will only be 20 on Opening Day. But in what will be another recurring theme this list cycle, it's still a lost year. And that inserts a bit more uncertainty into the profile.

Variance: High, bordering on extreme due to the lost developmental time and swing-and-miss concerns. He's a high ceiling/low floor prospect, with a wide swath of outcomes in between. We'll know a lot more this time next year ... hopefully (ominous orchestral stinger), after Robinson has spent a full season at ... well, full-season, but his upside isn't that far off Julio Rodriguez's.

Mark Barry's Fantasy Take: First list, first prospect, first taste of hyperbole. There's a chance Robinson is what we thought Jo Adell might be. Obviously it's early on Adell, but his five-tool potential is seriously tainted by a case of the whiffs. Robinson has flashed better plate discipline than Adell on his rise through the minors, and he has stolen more bases. Pair those attributes with a career line of .281/.366/.474 and we're heading into top-prospect-in-the-game territory. It's upside with an absolute Capital "U". Nice little start here.

───── ★ ★ ★ *2021 Top 101 Prospect* **#34** ★ ★ ★ ─────

2 **Corbin Carroll OF**   OFP: 60   ETA: Late 2022/Early 2023
Born: 08/21/00   Age: 20   Bats: L   Throws: L   Height: 5'10"   Weight: 165
Origin: Round 1, 2019 Draft (#16 overall)

The Report: "If he were two inches taller and 20 pounds heavier" is usually the introductory clause for a short right-handed pitcher we like more than we should. It applies to Carroll as well. If he were 6-foot—or at least tall enough to be listed at 6-foot—and a lean 185 or so, he wouldn't have slid to Arizona's 16th-overall pick last year. Everything else here points to a top-10 prep outfield pick, a potential plus speed/power combo for a likely major-league center fielder.

Development Track: There's an alternate history—are you sick of this yet—where Carroll torched both A-ball levels and made a jump from just off the 2020 Top 101 … well, into the meaty part where he will reside in the 2021 edition. A half dozen, maybe more, prospects make that jump every year. What would it have looked like? A .300 batting average, surprising power on contact given his frame, good defense in center field? There was enough of that present at Salt River Fields to justify the jump anyway, despite not having the Midwest and Cal League looks that would have laid that bare. And frankly, we were probably too low on Carroll last year due to his size. There's less upside than Robinson, but a bit more surety in the hit tool.

Variance: High. It's a collection of 55 or 60s on the scouting sheet, but when you line them all up in a center fielder, the overall profile should play up. On the other hand if it all falls a half grade short, there isn't a carrying tool and you just have an okay regular. And we are still a ways away from feeling too comfortable divining either of those outcomes.

Mark Barry's Fantasy Take: By now you're aware that steals are pretty hard to come by in fantasy circles, and Carroll offers a sweet, sweet blend of speed and a knack for getting on base that gives him a "Better Adam Eaton" upside. If that surprising power on contact holds, or dare I say, improves, he could be considerably more than that, but either way, Carroll is a top-20ish dynasty prospect for me.

───── ★ ★ ★ *2021 Top 101 Prospect* **#47** ★ ★ ★ ─────

3 **Alek Thomas CF**   OFP: 60   ETA: 2022
Born: 04/28/00   Age: 21   Bats: L   Throws: L   Height: 5'11"   Weight: 175
Origin: Round 2, 2018 Draft (#63 overall)

The Report: Hmm, perhaps the Diamondbacks have a type. Here's the third of the troika of center fielders who make loud contact. Thomas slots in between Carroll and Robinson in terms of physicality—although 99 percent of prospects are gonna slot behind Robinson in that respect—and his swing is geared more for the gaps than for over-the-fence power at present. It's plus raw though, and he's a plus athlete who might end up the center fielder of the group if all three find themselves on the same Diamondbacks roster.

Development Track: Thomas still has a very pretty left-handed swing with some power projection, and is the most likely of this group to be exactly a role-55 outfielder. That's not just because he's actually seen a fair bit of full-season ball. His is a more advanced game on both sides of the ball, and he's likely to be a passable regular even if the offensive profile plays more to averagish against better arms, but there is some hit-tool risk which isn't ideal for a profile that is also hit-tool driven. However, we think he will hit, and in a normal year, we might have seen him on the cusp of the majors by this point.

Variance: High. Thomas has more tangible pro experience than Robinson or Carroll, but it's not *a lot* of pro experience and it's a more batting-average-reliant profile, so you will want to see how the bat plays in the upper minors.

Mark Barry's Fantasy Take: You know, there's an alternate history where—oh you've heard that before? Fine.

His ceiling isn't quite as high as the other two ultra-talented center field prospects in this system, but that's akin to saying strawberry is the third-best Neapolitan ice cream flavor. That's still pretty good. I have a little less faith in Thomas's efficiency on the bases, which is the separator between him and Carroll for me, but Thomas is a no-doubt top-35 guy in my estimation.

★ ★ ★ *2021 Top 101 Prospect* **#90** ★ ★ ★

4

Geraldo Perdomo SS OFP: 60   ETA: 2022. 2021 is in play though.
Born: 10/22/99   Age: 21   Bats: S   Throws: R   Height: 6'2"   Weight: 185
Origin: International Free Agent, 2016

The Report: Perdomo more than held his own as a teenager at two A-ball stops in 2019 and slotted toward the back of last year's 101 on the strength of his advanced two-way profile. The offensive performance was mostly approach-driven, which can become a problem when upper minors pitchers start to challenge you, but he should be able to sting the ball enough to keep better arms honest. And Perdomo doesn't have to hit a ton, as he's a slick fielding shortstop who does everything well, if nothing spectacularly.

Development Track: We don't really have reason to move Perdomo much one direction or the other. He has a fairly stable, high-floor profile even with the missing year of minor league baseball. Generally, I'd think we'd argue the few months off would be more deleterious to hitters than pitchers, but Perdomo will enter 2021 in High-A or Double-A as a 21-year-old with some track record of pro performance and solid enough alternate site reports. How much power comes next season and beyond will determine whether or not the modifier "glove-first" gets tagged to his profile going forward. That profile is still likely to be that of a useful regular, though.

Variance: Medium. The defensive tools give Perdomo a high floor, as even if he settles in as an OBP-driven 90 DRC+ type, the glove should be good enough to make him an average regular. There is upside in the bat if he fills out and adds a bit of power, but his ceiling is likely lower overall than the names above him.

Mark Barry's Fantasy Take: I love this system.

I also love high-contact dudes who also have a knack for getting on base. As a pro, all Perdomo has done is hit, and when he's not hitting, he's working walks. Even without the possibility of power, he's one of my favorite under-21 guys in the minor leagues, but if he matures into a little pop, we're looking at a legit, five-category contributor.

5 **Bryce Jarvis RHP**   OFP: 60   ETA: Second half 2022
Born: 12/26/97   Age: 23   Bats: L   Throws: R   Height: 6'2"   Weight: 195
Origin: Round 1, 2020 Draft (#18 overall)

The Report: Prior to 2020, Jarvis was a scrawny back-of-the-weekend pitcher for Duke with advanced secondary pitches and command. What was lacking was an at-least average fastball, as his was typically scraping 90 mph. Jarvis needed to add several extra ticks to help his off-speed pitches get further separation off each other. Fast forward to this past spring and the fastball is now 92-95 with movement, command, and control all paired with two breaking balls flashing above average and a changeup that is easily plus or better. The added arm strength is visible in the rest of his body, with a highly athletic frame and delivery.

Development Track: The jump between his first two years on campus to his draft-eligible year was seismic. College hitters always had trouble against his spin and arm speed, so taking that next great leap with the fastball is what got him into the first round. The question many evaluators have is whether the velo bump is real and sustainable. This next year of development will be pivotal—not only in regards to maintaining this year's gains, but also to determining how much more can be added on his projectable body.

Variance: Medium. With no history of arm trouble and fluid mechanics, there is no reason to assume there is an impending injury around the corner even when factoring in the spike on the heater. Still, it's always a baked-in concern in the background. The great separators are the unteachable traits of his secondary pitches which should keep him a starter long-term.

Mark Barry's Fantasy Take: OK, so maybe I jumped the gun on my unconditional love for this system. And that's not a knock on Jarvis, at least not really. The improvements during his stint in college are super intriguing, but a righty with middling velocity typically is just another translation for a mid-to-back-end starter, which is definitely not as exciting. I'll take a flyer with a late-first or early second-round FYPD pick, but Jarvis isn't someone I'm immediately targeting.

6 Blake Walston   LHP   OFP: 60   ETA: 2023
Born: 06/28/01   Age: 20   Bats: L   Throws: L   Height: 6'5"   Weight: 175
Origin: Round 1, 2019 Draft (#26 overall)

The Report: I wasn't in the room for the Starling Marte trade discussions, but I can see why perhaps the D'backs may have been more willing to part with Brennan Malone than Walston. We preferred Malone over Walston a smidge last year on present stuff, but Walston had more upside due to his projectability and potential plus fastball/curve combo as a southpaw.

Development Track: Walston's velocity and changeup remain inconsistent. The frame remains projectable. He has reportedly added a slider to give a second breaking ball look. The lost development year still stings but, as noted in the Perdomo blurb, it stings less for pitchers and Walston still would have gotten his work in and received hands-on coaching in terms of stuff development. You'd have liked to see the slider in game action, and see how the fastball velocity held up across six innings on a cold night in the Midwest League, but the projection remains, and we remain bullish on a mid-rotation profile.

Variance: High. With all the added complexity in evaluation and ranking prospects in 2020, it's nice for one of these to just be able to fall back on "needs to consolidate plus fastball velocity and make change and command gains." It's like catching up with an old friend.

Mark Barry's Fantasy Take: Mid-rotation upside with high variance is not really the stuff of fantasy legend. Walston probably needs to be rostered in leagues of 200 prospects or more, but his present skill set should be fairly replicable on the waiver wire.

7 Corbin Martin   RHP   OFP: 55   ETA: Debuted in 2019
Born: 12/28/95   Age: 25   Bats: R   Throws: R   Height: 6'2"   Weight: 228
Origin: Round 2, 2017 Draft (#56 overall)

The Report: Martin is your standard polished, four-pitch college arm without obviously plus stuff. There is no weakness in the arsenal. He can run the fastball into the mid-90s, show you a couple different breaking ball looks, and has an advanced, above-average changeup. Martin cruised through the minors (although the performance probably stopped short of "dominant") but everything pointed to a safeish, mid-rotation arm, and he made it to the majors less than two years after he was drafted. Then Martin tore his UCL and needed Tommy John surgery. Then he was traded to the Diamondbacks as part of the Zack Greinke deal. "Safeish" doesn't mean safe.

Development Track: Martin was functionally on rehab at the alternate site and was throwing without restriction within those parameters. The fastball velocity is back to mid-90s and was there for multi-inning stints. Assuming no major setbacks this offseason or next spring, he should be ready to go for Opening Day, and while he may not break camp with the big club, a healthy Martin is a major-league ready starter.

Variance: Medium. Martin's recovery from Tommy John surgery hasn't had any real red flags yet. But recovery isn't "recovered" and until we see how the stuff plays in longer stints in real game action, there's going to be additional health and profile risk.

Mark Barry's Fantasy Take: For my money, I'll take Martin as the top fantasy hurler in this org. If mid-rotation is the upside, give me the guy who's the closest and has flashed the ability to look fairly decent against big-league hitters (minus giving up eight dingers in 19 1/3 innings—that's, uh, less than ideal). Factor in his return from Tommy John surgery, and you might have a guy who's flying a little below the radar this offseason. As an aside, if your league gives extra points for dudes named Corbin, this is the system for you.

8. Slade Cecconi   RHP

OFP: 60   ETA: Late 2022 as a starter, early 2022 as a reliever
Born: 06/24/99   Age: 22   Bats: R   Throws: R   Height: 6'4"   Weight: 219
Origin: Round 1, 2020 Draft (#33 overall)

The Report: Cecconi ranked 30th on our pre-draft big board due to his prototypical starting pitcher's frame and big fastball/slider combo. As a draft-eligible sophomore he didn't have a long college track record, and might have been able to move into the top half of the first round with a full ACC campaign where he showed off a more complete arsenal along with the ability to log innings and throw good strikes. But all in all there's more upside with Cecconi than your median supplemental round college arm.

Development Track: Cecconi was up into the high-90s in short bursts at the alternate site. He paired the fastball with a potential plus slider and showed a full four-pitch mix. He's a potential breakout arm in 2021 if he continues to refine his secondaries and manages to log 100+ healthy innings as a starter.

Variance: Medium. Cecconi will have to show he can hold up under a starter's workload because he has had arm issues and was used fairly conservatively as a freshman at Miami. He will also need to develop the curve and/or change as well to avoid the fallback position of power fastball/slider reliever.

Mark Barry's Fantasy Take: On the one hand, pairing arm issues with a predominantly two-pitch mix sure screams reliever. On the other, those two pitches are good enough to give Cecconi a pretty exciting ceiling should the changeup or curve develop into legit offerings. Outside the top-100, I'm more likely to chase the upside on an arm like Cecconi than settle for a back-end starter.

9 **Seth Beer 1B**   OFP: 55   ETA: 2021
Born: 09/18/96   Age: 24   Bats: L   Throws: R   Height: 6'3"   Weight: 225
Origin: Round 1, 2018 Draft (#28 overall)

The Report: Beer has been a well-known prospect since he was one of the best offensive players in college baseball as a true freshman at Clemson in 2016. That made him an early 1.1 candidate for the 2018 draft, and he's never quite lived up to it since. Still, he has a fantastic plate approach, and the potential for plus hit/plus power. There's more swing-and-miss than you'd hope for given the rest of the offensive profile. Defensively … well, he has "versatility" in the sense that he can stand at first or in the outfield and catch most of what's aimed directly at him, but the best fit here is at DH. He'll get as far as his bat carries him.

Development Track: We got surprisingly strong positive feedback on Beer from the alternate site. On the flip side, he didn't show up in the majors despite spending most of 2019 in Double-A and the unexpected availability of DH at-bats. We think the arrow is pointing up a little, and the likelihood of a permanent NL DH spot certainly helps the long-term value.

Variance: Medium. The hitting profile in and of itself is low variance. But the lack of secondary value past his bat means that even if Beer falls just a moderate amount short, he's more likely to be a Triple-A (or KBO) superstar than a major-league role player.

Mark Barry's Fantasy Take: If this were a pure fantasy list, Beer would probably check in at number five, just behind Perdomo. His power, plate discipline, and lack of defensive position is very Kyle Schwarber-y, even if all of Beer's offerings are a notch below. As a guy whose defensive role is "Lol, no thanks", he'll need the DH to stick in the NL or a trade to an American League team to reach his full potential, but he hits and has always hit. He's going to need to in order to be useful as a fantasy option, or else he might not get enough run to really matter.

10 **Levi Kelly RHP**   OFP: 55   ETA: Late 2021 as a reliever, Late 2022 as a starter.
Born: 05/14/99   Age: 22   Bats: R   Throws: R   Height: 6'4"   Weight: 205
Origin: Round 8, 2018 Draft (#249 overall)

The Report: Kelly jumped as a pitching prospect in 2019 in full-season ball, showing a plus fastball/slider combo that usually overpowered Midwest League lineups. Improved mechanics gave him a better shot to start, while the two-pitch combo provided a solid relief fallback.

Development Track: Well, if anything the slider might be even better now, and Kelly's stuff played against much more advanced hitters at the alternate site. The rest of the arsenal still lags behind, but it's 2021 and your starting pitching projection is determined less by the quality of your third pitch than the quality of your best two.

Variance: Medium. Given the potential plus-plus slider, Kelly could break camp in the Diamondbacks' bullpen, spam that pitch 40 percent of the time, and find immediate major-league success. And major-league teams are much more willing to take a pitcher with two really good pitches and let them start than they were a decade ago. That all said, Kelly hasn't pitched above A-ball, and has the usual third pitch and command concerns. So I'm going to note there is significant reliever risk even considering the potential reliever impact.

Mark Barry's Fantasy Take: Kelly is probably a reliever, and it takes an awful lot to be fantasy relevant from the 'pen. That slider is going to need to be really, really good.

The Prospects You Meet Outside The Top Ten:

Prospects who might be Top Ten in a shallower system

Tommy Henry **LHP** Born: 07/29/97 Age: 23 Bats: L Throws: L Height: 6'3" Weight: 205 Origin: Round 2, 2019 Draft (#74 overall)

The former Michigan Man's velocity jumped a bit in the spring before everything shut down, scraping the mid-90s now, and he held it at the alternate site. The changeup was already above-average coming out of college, and the breaking balls are improving too. Combine that with his already strong command profile, and his stock is moving up. Even though his entire pro career is only three innings in short-season ball, Henry could be a rotation option as early as 2021.

Luis Frias **RHP** Born: 05/23/98 Age: 23 Bats: R Throws: R Height: 6'3" Weight: 180 Origin: International Free Agent, 2015

Frias might end up in "major-league-ready arms, but probably relievers" group a year or so down the line, but given the size and plus fastball/curve combo, there's no reason to rush the transition. He also has feel for a developing split as the third pitch, but the bigger hurdle to starting might be the sheer length of limbs Frias has to corral in his delivery. The fastball could play in the upper-90s in relief though, and the curve is a nasty 12-6 downer to pair with it in short bursts.

Prospects to dream on a little

Wilderd Patino **CF** Born: 07/18/01 Age: 19 Bats: R Throws: R Height: 6'1" Weight: 175 Origin: International Free Agent, 2017

Patino's upside isn't that far off Carroll and Thomas, due to big time raw power out of a frame that can stick in center field—at least for now. The lost developmental year hits hard here as he needs to make strides with his hit tool and general swing-and-miss, and that would have been best served by 140 games against age-appropriate competition.

Jeferson Espinal CF Born: 06/07/02   Age: 19   Bats: L   Throws: L   Height: 6'0"   Weight: 180   Origin: International Free Agent, 2018

Espinal is a safe—and potential plus—center fielder, as he's a true top-of-the-scale burner. There is some potential at the plate as well, but it's mostly projection outside of an already-advanced-for-his-age approach, and the overall tool kit isn't as loud as Patino's.

Safe MLB bats, but less upside than you'd like

Pavin Smith 1B Born: 02/06/96   Age: 25   Bats: L   Throws: L   Height: 6'2"   Weight: 210   Origin: Round 1, 2017 Draft (#7 overall)

At this point, Smith is unlikely to reach the heights with the bat that would justify taking a college first baseman seventh overall, but he is a disciplined hitter who could give you .270 with plenty of walks and some pull side pop. He has started playing some corner outfield and runs well enough to handle it, although he's a bit awkward on the grass at present. He's an above-average first baseman. Smith is a useful lefty bench bat who could spend a few years as an average regular if he more consistently taps into the pull side power.

Stuart Fairchild OF Born: 03/17/96   Age: 25   Bats: R   Throws: R   Height: 6'0"   Weight: 200   Origin: Round 2, 2017 Draft (#38 overall)

Acquired from the Reds as part of the Archie Bradley trade, Fairchild is a pretty safe bet to get some major-league run due to his plus center field glove and ability to hit left-handed pitching, but the profile likely tops out as a good fourth outfielder.

Dominic Fletcher CF Born: 09/02/97   Age: 23   Bats: L   Throws: L   Height: 5'9"   Weight: 185   Origin: Round 2, 2019 Draft (#75 overall)

Fletcher and Fairchild are a bit of a matched set. The likely outcome for both is fourth outfielder, and Fletcher is merely decent in center. But there's upside in the bat—and underrated pop—that is more likely to carry him to a regular role. He's also further away, so order the profiles how you like.

MLB-ready arms, but probably relievers

J.B. Bukauskas RHP Born: 10/11/96   Age: 24   Bats: R   Throws: R   Height: 6'0"   Weight: 210   Origin: Round 1, 2017 Draft (#15 overall)

Bukauskas has had durability and command issues dating back to his college days at North Carolina. He's still likely to be a reliever, but he is healthy now and showing two plus secondaries (change and slider) to go with his plus-plus heat. It's potential closer stuff as soon as Opening Day 2021.

Jon Duplantier RHP Born: 07/11/94   Age: 26   Bats: L   Throws: R   Height: 6'4"   Weight: 240   Origin: Round 3, 2016 Draft (#89 overall)

Duplantier has had durability and command issues dating back to his college days at Rice. He's still likely to be a reliever, but he is healthy now, and has a power fastball/breaker combo that could make him a late-inning reliever as soon as Opening Day 2021.

Taylor Widener **RHP** Born: 10/24/94 Age: 26 Bats: L Throws: R Height: 6'0" Weight: 230 Origin: Round 12, 2016 Draft (#368 overall)

Widener has not had recent durability issues, pitching more than 100 innings every year from 2017-2019. He hit a wall as a starter in the PCL West with Reno—happens to the best of us, especially with the 2019 Triple-A ball—and the Diamondbacks moved him to the 'pen where he was a (high spin) 95-and-a-slider reliever for the big club in 2020. It's late-inning stuff if he can refine his command and find more consistency with the razorblade, mid-80s breaker.

Humberto Mejía **RHP** Born: 03/03/97 Age: 24 Bats: R Throws: R Height: 6'4" Weight: 235 Origin: International Free Agent, 2013

Mejia has a better chance to be a starter then the names above—and has already made MLB starts—but might fit best as a 95-and-a-curve reliever. He's going to be 24 and hadn't pitched in the upper minors yet when the Marlins called him up to soak up starts. The delivery is effortful enough I think he fits best maxing out in a setup role, but Mejia has a solid frame and will show you four pitches. You might develop a fourth starter with further minor league reps, but he doesn't have the same late-inning upside as the rest of this group if he does end up in the 'pen.

Top Talents 25 and Under (as of 4/1/2021):

1. Zac Gallen, RHP
2. Kristian Robinson, OF
3. Corbin Carroll, OF
4. Alex Thomas, OF
5. Daulton Varsho, C/OF
6. Geraldo Perdomo, SS
7. Bryce Jarvis, RHP
8. Blake Walston, LHP
9. Corbin Martin, RHP
10. Slade Cecconi, RHP

Once again, Zac Gallen was a very good major-league pitcher in 2020. His ERA has outshined his DRA since he's been called up, and between his 2019 midseason call-up and the shortened 2020 season, he's only done this for 152 innings. Yet it's 152 innings of a No. 2 starter, and nothing seems wildly unsustainable. Gallen throws four pitches, misses bats, and has been quite durable over his pro career.

He might "only" be a No. 3 moving forward if he regresses a bit, but that's still a heck of a pitching talent, and we're pretty confident he's at least going to be that good.

Daulton Varsho is the first player we've mentioned who lost their rookie eligibility when MLB amended its own rules at the end of the season to include September service time for the 2020 season only. After internal discussion, we went with the MLB rule, and Varsho was 29 at-bats short of exhausting his eligibility but tipped over on service time when including September days. We still get to talk about him (and most of the rest of this cohort) in our 25U writeups, though.

Arizona used Varsho in a third catcher/superutility type role the first half of the season, playing once a week for Carson Kelly and Stephen Vogt behind the plate while also seeing time in the outfield and DH. After Starling Marte was traded to Miami, he slowly took over semi-regular center field duties, while also still catching once or twice a week. It was an unusual deployment for an unusually speedy catcher in an organization with a young major-league starter ahead of him. At the plate, he struggled to hit for average, though he came on late after settling into a more regular role. The long-term defensive home is still unsettled, and it might not be easy to define, but we think he'll bring value and versatility to a club for a long time to come.

Part 3: Featured Articles

Diamondbacks All-Time Top 10 Players

by Steven Goldman

POSITION PLAYERS

MIGUEL MONTERO, C (2006-2014)
He emerged as a prospect as more of an offensive catcher than a promising defender. Reaching the majors, he didn't hit at first but his glove endeared itself to Randy Johnson during his late-career encore with the team. Impatient at the plate, he gradually became more selective and peaked from 2009-2012, hitting .283/.361/.457 in those years. The Diamondbacks and then-GM Kevin Towers signed him to a five-year, $60 million contract extension in May of '12. It was the largest contract in team history to that point, and it didn't work out—Montero hit .237/.324/.358 over the next two years and was traded to the Cubs for Zack Godley and Jeferson Mejia.

PAUL GOLDSCHMIDT, 1B (2011-2018)
Those tempted to mourn the old days when the greats spend their whole careers with one team should be reminded that it wasn't up to them then and it often isn't up to them now. Thus does the best player in Diamondbacks history find himself finishing out his career in St. Louis. To get a sense of how good Goldschmidt has been consider the competition: Freddie Freeman got his first cup of coffee in 2010 but became a regular in 2011; Goldschmidt, Anthony Rizzo, and Eric Hosmer came up in 2011. The tale of the tape:

	G	RATES	OPS+	WARP	OTHER
Hosmer	1403	.278/.336/.435	108	13.1	4 GGs
Freeman	1406	.295/.383/.509	139	29.1	1 GG, 2020 MVP
Rizzo	1265	.271/.372/.475	129	29.4	4 GGs
Goldschmidt	1311	.293/.392/.522	141	39.3	3 GGs

The Diamondbacks avoided having to pay Goldschmidt for his declining years by dealing him at the end of their last contract, and that's a defensible move from a value standpoint. In every other sense it's an abject loss.

KETEL MARTE, 2B/SS/OF (2017-PRESENT)
When the Mariners traded Marte to the D'Backs they must have told themselves they were dispensing with a light-hitting middle infielder, sans patience or power and unlikely to develop any. They were wrong, although it's unclear just how far off they were given the way Marte's 2019 is, so far, an outlier in his career. His .329/.389/.592, 32-homer season looks as if it beamed in from another player's career. If it remains a one-off, Arizona still has a versatile player who can run and isn't an automatic out at the plate. The other guy is a Hall of Famer. Stay tuned.

STEPHEN DREW, SS (2006-2012)
All three Drew brothers, J.D., Tim, and Stephen, were first-round draft picks (in 1997 and 1998, 1997, and 2004, respectively); geneticists ought to be collecting blood samples from Mr. and Mrs. Drew to see if what they had together can be bottled. Stephen was almost as hyped as J.D. was. "Observers liken him to a hybrid, crossing Mark Teixeira with Alex Rodriguez," we reported in late 2004. What those observers had been drinking has yet to be established, but whatever it was it clouded their judgment: Drew was not a coming star. At his best he was a solid contributor. Away from Chase Field he hit .258/.315/.417 (it was .274/.343/.456 at home), respectable numbers for a shortstop who was a solid defender, if far from elite.

STEVE FINLEY, OF (1999-2003)
He had a unique career, with offensive numbers that were all over the map. He hit all of 10 home runs in a 225-game minor league run and averaged seven per 162 games played during his first four seasons in the majors, but had slugged 304 of them by the time he retired, including a career-high 36 at 39 years old. At 27, normally around peak age, he hit five in 162 games. He was an International League batting champion but averaged only .271, peaking at .298. He maintained a reputation as an elite defensive player well past the point it was true, then rediscovered his range in Arizona. The Diamondbacks signed him at about the point most players are getting ready to quit and got some of the best years of his career as well as excellent play throughout the 2001 postseason run. He legged out 12 triples when he was 41. Some of the changes he went through were attributable to the way the game's offensive levels were redefined upwards during his career, but some of it was that he was just an odd specimen.

LUIS GONZALEZ, OF (1999-2006)

Much like Finley, he started out as one thing and turned himself into another. Playing with the Cubs and Astros through his 29th birthday he hit .268/.342/.425, and 15 home runs counted as a big year. "In each of the past two years," The Scouting Notebook: 1998 opined, "he's played for teams that have asked him to be a run-producer, when he's really everything but one." By that the author meant that he was a good outfield glove-man who hit a little. From then through the end of his career 11 years later Gonzalez hit .291/.380/.509 with 270 home runs including one of the great out-of-nowhere seasons, his 2001 with the Diamondbacks: .325/.429/.688 with 57 home runs. As we wrote in 2004, just as he was exiting that unexpected late peak, "It's a five-year stretch as a Hall of Fam hitter tacked onto the back end of a mediocre career." And all the Diamondbacks had to do to get it was trade Karim Garcia to the Tigers.

CHRIS YOUNG, OF (2006-2012)

A power-speed combination seemingly out of the 1980s, Young began his professional career in the White Sox organization but was traded to the Diamondbacks in December 2005 to obtain pitcher Javier Vazquez. Prior to the 2007 season, we called him the eighth-best prospect in all of baseball while Baseball America ranked him at no. 12. The reality didn't match the hype. Young did come close to reaching the 30-30 mark in several campaigns but had so much swing and miss in his game that he struggled to get his batting average out of the .230s. Same-side pitchers were a special problem, holding him to .225/.295/.413 rates throughout his career. He offset the low averages with good power (not just home runs but doubles), walks, stolen bases, and good defense. He made some of his greatest contributions to the D'Backs in the postseason, hitting five home runs in 12 games.

JUSTIN UPTON, OF (2007-2012)

The D'Backs made Upton the first-overall pick of the 2005 draft but never seemed all that happy with the choice or with him. Upton, we said around the time of his pro debut, had "more tools than Home Depot." He made it to the majors as a teen, hit .300 at 21, and hit over 30 home runs for the first time at 23. He was also frustratingly inconsistent, hitting only 17 home runs in 2010 and 2012. Some of the variability was attributable to injuries, but even after he was traded to the Braves in January of 2013 he continued to be unpredictable, for example hitting 12 home runs in April of that season, then only four in the next three months combined. Relations between player and team had soured long before the deal, with inevitably team-sourced innuendo about his work ethic circulating as early as 2006. Going on 16 years after Upton was drafted, he occupies a strangely liminal space between journeyman and star who was not who he was predicted to be but didn't fail either.

AJ POLLOCK, OF (2012-2018)

The 17th-overall pick of the 2009 draft (taken seven picks before fellow piscine player Mike Trout, alas), Pollock proved to be a valuable player during his D'Backs tenure, displaying an odd combination of skills, sort of a little but of everything, but not too much of any one of them. The one skill he consistently failed to display was good health, cresting the 500-plate appearance mark just once, in 2015. He was at his best that year, hitting .315/.367/.498 in 157 games, making his sole All-Star team to date and picking up his only Gold Glove. Arizona being in an austerity mode, his departure as a free agent was preordained, but given his friability and declining speed it was probably a wise choice regardless.

DAVID PERALTA, OF (2014-Present)

It's almost the Roy Hobbs story minus the violence: Signed out of Venezuela, Peralta was given a brief trial as a pitcher in the Cardinals organization as a teen. Multiple shoulder surgeries ensued. Four years later he reappeared as an outfielder with the independent Rio Grande Valley WhiteWings of the North American League. He continued to rake with the independent Wichita Wingnuts of the American Association, a performance which got him an invitation to join the Diamondbacks at High-A Visalia. He was 25 years old, old for the level, but he still hit his way to the big leagues. Since then he's logged such achievements as leading the NL in triples and hitting 30 home runs. It is stories like Peralta's that an expansive, vibrant minor leagues makes possible.

PITCHERS

RANDY JOHNSON, LHP (1999-2004, 2007-2008)

Johnson was such an awe-inspiring specimen he almost needs to be described in Biblical terms. "It was then… that the Nephilim appeared on earth—when the divine beings cohabited with the daughters of men, who bore them offspring. They were the heroes of old, then of renown." Johnson was already 35 when he signed with the Diamondbacks but his peak was yet to come. He had five seasons of over 10 WARP and all of them came during his first stint with the team. In those half-dozen years, which included one subpar half-season due to knee problems, he went 103-49 with a 2.65 ERA, pitched as many as 271.2 innings, allowed only 7.1 hits per nine innings, walked only 359 batters and struck out 1,832. He passed the 300-strikeout mark in four consecutive seasons and was recognized with four consecutive Cy Young Awards. If you haven't had enough superlatives, may we also mention that he carried the Diamondbacks during the 2001 postseason, going 5-1 with a 1.52 ERA in 41.1 innings and winning the World Series MVP award having started twice as well as coming out of the bullpen to Win Game 7? Six-foot-10 with a wingspan to match, his slider coming at the batter from what must have felt like the first base stands, he resembled nothing so much as a predatory bird, Titanus of Arizona. There will be other great pitchers, but we won't see Johnson's like again.

BYUNG-HYUN KIM, RHP (1999-2003, 2007)
A sidearmer somewhat rushed to the majors, Kim fought wildness for years, walking 5.1 batters per nine innings during his first three seasons in the big leagues and 4.0 per nine for his career. That said, he was extremely hard to hit during this period, particularly for same-side hitters: Right-handed batters averaged .185/.278/.295 during this initial D'Backs phase. Lefties had an easier time, but only in relative terms, hitting .212/.338/.343. It all came together in 2001-2002, with Kim throwing 182 innings, allowing just 122 hits, walking 70, and striking out 205 with an ERA of 2.52. Kim's poor showing in the 2001 World Series seemingly didn't hurt him going forward, but what did was his desire to start rather than close. Dealt to the Red Sox in part to pursue that dream, Kim saw scant success from then on, turning in a 5.07 career ERA as a starter versus 3.58 as a reliever.

CURT SCHILLING, RHP (2000-2003)
Schilling was traded by the Red Sox, Orioles, and Astros before establishing himself as a star with the Phillies. Nearly 30 when he made it to the other side of the injury nexus and found consistency, he struck out over 300 batters in consecutive seasons. He was aided in this by the addition of a split-fingered fastball to his arsenal and a heavy workload enabled by a seemingly intimidated manager Terry Francona who allowed him to pile up innings and complete games. Once he found himself he pitched with an extraordinary combination of great stuff and impeccable command, leading the NL in strikeout-walk ratio five times. In 2002, when he was 35, he walked 33 batters in 259.1 innings while striking out 316 for a strikeout-walk ratio of 9.58. It was then the second-best showing in that category in history. He was also one of the greatest postseason pitchers, going 11-2 with a 2.23 ERA in 19 starts and sharing the 2001 World Series MVP with Randy Johnson after allowing just four runs in 21.1 innings. He walked only two and struck out 26. He pitched with such great intelligence that it makes his post-career habit of willful obtuseness and chronic mendacity even more difficult to tolerate than it otherwise would be.

MIGUEL BATISTA, RHP (2001-2004, 2006)
Batista pitched better for the Diamondbacks than he did anywhere else on a peripatetic journey through the major leagues. After scuffling through his 20s, he was well utilized in a swingman role in 2001 but was less consistent as a full-time starter in subsequent years. He was very good again in 2003, posting a 3.54 ERA in 193.1 innings while walking only 60, striking out 142, and inducing grounders. He once credited his Arizona improvement to increased concentration on the

mound, which was unusually candid, and in his spare time wrote poetry and fiction. There's something wonderful about a pitcher who was a journeyman on the mound but a renaissance man otherwise.

BRANDON WEBB, RHP (2003-2009)
The Hall of Fame voting rules set a lower boundary of 10 years of major league service for eligibility, though they've bent it on occasion, such as for Deadball-Era hurler Addie Joss, who died in midcareer having made it through not quite nine full seasons. Webb didn't make it all the way through six before shoulder injuries ended his career at 30, but his five years of health were a period of sustained excellence—even if the won-lost records didn't always show it. A ground-ball machine who also gets strikeouts leaves batters few ways to win. Webb was, as we wrote in 2004, "a sinkerballer of absurd ability;" though his fastball sat only in the 89-91-mph range, he used it exceedingly well. He was just peaking as his career ended: His ERAs were always good, but it took him until his third season to get full command of his arsenal. From 2005 through 2008 he went 70-37 with a 3.23 ERA. He won the 2006 Cy Young Award, was runner-up in 2007 and 2008, and that was all she wrote.

DAN HAREN, RHP (2008-2010)
Haren's career ended in a long journeyman phase in which he pitched with only intermittent effectiveness for the Angels, Nationals, Dodgers, Marlins, and Cubs, but to that point in his career he'd pitched to a 3.59 ERA (119 ERA+) over nine years. He was also highly durable, making at least 30 starts every year from 2005 through the end of his career in 2015. A second-round pick by the St. Louis Cardinals out of Pepperdine University, Haren was given a couple of brief trials by the big-league club before being packaged off to Oakland in return for Mark Mulder. He had two good years for the A's before being traded again, this time to the Diamondbacks. He only stayed for two years and change before being dealt again, this time to the Angels, but he gave Arizona the two best years of his career. Haren's hallmark was great control and he led the NL in strikeout-walk ratio in both of his full seasons, passing just 78 batters while striking out 429 in 445.1 innings. As we wrote in 2010, "On pure stuff, durability, control, command, track record, age and contract status, one would be hard-pressed to find five more valuable pitchers in the entire sport." His July 2010 trade to Anaheim returned another pitcher on this list, Patrick Corbin.

IAN KENNEDY, RHP (2010-2013)
A former first-round pick who wore out his welcome with the Yankees by not being sufficiently contrite following some bad outings, he was sent west as part of the three-team trade that sent Max Scherzer to Detroit and Curtis Granderson to New York. A "polished college pitcher," Kennedy had a low ceiling and a high floor, which is to say he didn't throw hard but he knew what to do with what

he had. Another pitcher in the D'Backs tradition of throwing strikes, Kennedy limited his walks to 2.2 per nine in his peak season of 2011, going 21-4 with a 2.88 ERA. He finished fourth in the Cy Young Award voting that fall. Consistency eluded him after that—note that, though still active in the major leagues as of this writing, he has yet to receive even a down-ballot mention in another Cy Young vote. It wouldn't be fair to call Kennedy a one-hit wonder, and yet that season hinted at gifts that would never be received. He was traded to the Padres at the 2013 deadline for Matt Stites and Joe Thatcher. Ah, the Kevin Towers years.

PATRICK CORBIN, LHP (2012-2018)

Corbin, we wrote in 2017, is "blessed with boyish good looks and a devastating slider." He had the good looks all along, but the slider had to withstand 2014 Tommy John surgery—the slider is hard on the arm and Corbin throws his often. The timing was heartbreaking; Corbin had just emerged as a potential frontline pitcher the year before when he went 9-0 with a 1.98 ERA through his first 12 starts. It took a few years before he rediscovered the consistency that he had shown when he was 23, wrapping up his Diamondbacks stint with a 2018 that merited down-ballot Cy Young consideration with 246 strikeouts against only 48 walks in 2018 innings.

ROBBIE RAY, LHP (2015-2020)

Acquired by the Diamondbacks along with infielder Domingo Leyba in return for shortstop Didi Gregorius in the second of the team's significant three-way trades with the Yankees and Tigers, chaos-hurler Ray fought his command for years and, to borrow from Bobby Fuller, his command won. That's something of a cheap shot because he had periods of great effectiveness, particularly in 2017, when he went 15-5 with a 2.89 ERA and an NL-leading 12.1 strikeouts per nine innings. It was the second of what would be three 200-strikeout seasons in Arizona. Most importantly, he achieved it in a year interrupted by what could have been a fatal event—a 108-mph line drive off the bat of then-Cardinal Luke Voit which hit him in the back of the head. Somehow he avoided serious injury and returned in less than a month, continuing to pitch effectively. His next two seasons were solid as well, albeit at a lower level, but when his control unraveled again in 2020 the Diamondbacks dealt him in a hurry.

ZACK GREINKE, RHP (2016-2019)

Who was selected ahead of sixth-overall draft-pick Greinke in 2002? Bryan Bullington (Pirates), the then-B.J. Upton (Devil Rays), Chris Gruler (Reds), Adam Loewen (Orioles), and Clint Everts (Expos). That was a long time ago, and the Diamondback's decision to sign Greinke, whose left his best fastball in Los Angeles if not Kansas City, continued their record of betting on elder pitchers, provided those pitchers are among the greatest ever to pick up the horsehide sphere. After a rough first year with the team, he redefined himself yet again, reemphasizing a changeup he had begun to rely on towards the end his blue (read: Dodgers) period and going more often to his very slow curve. The six-year, $206.5 million contract the team offered to Greinke at 32 was excessive, provoking the deadline-day trade to the hungry Astros in 2019, but for 3.5 years the Diamondbacks gave their fans regular looks at a future Hall of Famer. It's more than the Pirates would have done.

A Taxonomy of 2020 Abnormalities

by Rob Mains

I'm going to start this with a trivia question. Trust me, it's relevant. Don't bother skipping to the end of the article to find the answer, it's not there.

Only five players have appeared in 140 or more games for 16 straight seasons. Who are they?

It's a trivia question starting off an essay, so you know how this works: Whatever you guessed, you're wrong. It's okay. As someone who purchased this book, chances are good that you're an educated baseball fan. But the circumstances behind 2020 force us to abandon, or at least seriously question, some of our favorite patterns and crutches for evaluating the game we love.

We just completed what was undoubtedly the strangest season in MLB history. No fans, geographically limited schedule, universal DH, seven-inning twin bills, runners on second in extra innings, a 16-team postseason, a club playing at a Triple-A stadium. Some of these changes will likely persist (sorry), but we've never had so many tweaks dumped on us all at once, at least not since they figured out how many balls were in a walk.

And the biggest, of course, was the 60-game season. The 19th century was dotted with teams that went bankrupt before the season ended, but the lone season with only 60 scheduled games was 1877. That year there were only six teams, the league rostered a total of 77 players (just 16 more than the 2020 Marlins), and batters called for pitches to be thrown high or low by the pitcher, who was 50 feet away. We can say the 2020 season was easily the shortest ever for recognizable baseball.

As such, it'll stand out. Few abbreviated seasons do. Just about everybody reading this knows the 1994 season ended after Seattle's Randy Johnson struck out Oakland's Ernie Young for the last out of the Mariners-A's game on August 11. The ensuing player strike wiped out the rest of the season and the postseason. Teams played only 112-117 games that year.

And many of you know that a strike in the middle of the 1981 season split the season in two, resulting in the only Division Series until 1995. Teams played only 103-111 games that year, the shortest regular season since 1885.

Those two seasons are memorable. So when we see that nobody drove in 100 runs in 1981, or that Greg Maddux was the only pitcher with 180 or more innings pitched in 1994, we think, "Of course. Strike year."

But we don't remember other short years. You might not recall that the 1994 strike spilled into the next year, chopping 18 games off the 1995 schedule. You might've read that the 1918 season, played during the last pandemic, ended after Labor Day due to the government's World War I "work or fight" order. A strike erased the first week and a half of the 1972 season, but that year's best known as the last time pitchers batted in the American League.

The point is, while we don't remember small changes to the schedule, we remember the big ones. The 1981 mid-season strike. The 1994 season- and Series-ending strike. And, of course, the pandemic-shortened 2020 season. We won't need a reminder why Marcell Ozuna's 18 homers were the fewest to lead the National League in a century. (Literally; Cy Williams led with 15 in 1920.)

Now, about that trivia question. The five players are Hank Aaron, Brooks Robinson, Pete Rose, Ichiro Suzuki, and Johnny Damon. The one nobody gets, of course, is Damon, and a lot of people miss Ichiro, whose last season of 140-plus games came garbed in the red-orange and ocean blue of Miami when he was 42. That's half of what makes it a good question. The other half is the two guys whom many think made the list but didn't. Lou Gehrig? His streak started in the Yankees' 42nd game of the 1925 season and lasted only 13 seasons after that. And everybody assumes Cal Ripken Jr. did it, having played 2,632 straight games over 17 seasons. But one of those 17 seasons was 1994, when the Orioles played only 112 games.

My point? *I just told you* everybody remembers the 1994 strike year, but everybody forgets it fell in the middle of Ripken's streak, separating the first twelve years from the last four. Just because we recall something doesn't mean it's always at the front of our minds.

Nobody is going to forget 2020, and baseball is obviously not the main reason. But there will come a time in the future when you're looking at a player's or a team's record, and there will be baffling numbers there for 2020, and you'll think, "I wonder what happened." (Not to mention the missing line for minor league players.) Just like you forgot that the 1994 strike limited Ripken to 112 games.

Try not to forget it, though. The 2020 season resulted in weird statistical results for several reasons.

There were only 60 games.
I know, duh. But that had impacts beyond counting stats like Ozuna's home run total or Yu Darvish and Shane Bieber leading the majors with eight wins. (I know, pitcher wins, but still.)

The 162-game season is the longest among major North American sports, and that duration gives us a gift. Over the course of a long season, small variations tend to even out. A player who has a ten-game hot streak will probably have a ten-game cold streak. A team that starts the year losing a bunch of close games will probably win a bunch of them. We get regression to the mean. Statistics stabilize.

Consider flipping a coin. Over the long run, we expect it to come up heads about half the time. But the fewer flips, the more variation there'll be. If you flip a coin six times, probability theory tells us you'll get at least two-third heads about 34 percent of the time. Flip it 30 times, your chance of two-thirds heads drops to five percent.

Or, relevant to this case, if you flip a coin 60 times, your chance of getting at least 36 heads—that's 60 percent—is 7.75 percent. Expand the coin-flipping to 162 times, and the chance of getting 60 percent heads drops to 0.73 percent.

In other words, the odds of an outcome that's 20 percent better (or worse) than expected is *more than ten times higher* when you flip your coin 60 times than when you do it 162 times. Call it small sample size, call lack of mean reversion, or call it luck not evening out, 162 is a lot more predictive than 60. You get much more variation over 60 games than over 162. Bieber's 1.63 ERA and 0.87 FIP aren't something we'd see over a full season, and neither is Javier Baéz's .203/.238/.360.

Some players' lines in 2020 look normal. Brian Anderson had an .811 OPS in 2019 and an .810 OPS in 2020. (He probably would have gotten that last point if he'd been given enough time.) But there are many like Bieber and Baéz, some of them from young players still establishing their talent levels. The answer to the question, "What went right or wrong for that guy in 2020?" is most likely "Nothing, it was just a 2020 thing."

Preseason training was abbreviated for hitters.

Every year, spring training drags. Players get tired of it, fans get tired of it, and you sure can tell sportswriters get tired of it. Yes, something to get everyone into shape is necessary, but does it really have to drag on for over a month? Can't we shorten it?

The 2020 season answered in the negative, at least for hitters. Warren Spahn is credited with saying that hitting is timing and pitching is upsetting timing. It appears nobody had his timing down after the abbreviated July summer camp. Through August 9—18 games into the season—MLB batters were hitting .230/.311/.395 with a .275 BABIP. That BABIP, had it held, would have been the lowest since 1968, the Year of the Pitcher. In recent years it's hovered around .300.

It didn't hold. Play returned to more normal levels the rest of the year: .249/.325/.425 with a .297 BABIP starting August 10. But batters whose play concentrated in those first two weeks wound up with ugly lines. Andrew

Benintendi went on the injured list with a season-ending rib cage strain on August 11. His final line: .103/.314/.128 in 14 games. Franchy Cordero went on the IL with a hamate bone fracture on August 9 and a .154/.185/.231 line. Even though he came back strong in a late September return, it was too late to repair his full-season numbers.

Preseason training was abbreviated for pitchers.

Every year, spring training drags. Players get tired of it, fans get tired of it … wait, I already said that. But the abbreviated preseason was tough on pitchers, too. As noted, they had the upper hand coming out of the gate. But then they lost that hand. And then their arms, too.

The 2020 season was spread over 67 days. During those 67 days, 237 pitchers hit the Injured List, compared to 135 in the first 67 days of 2019. A lot of those IL stints, though, were COVID-19-related. Still, over the first 67 days of the 2019 season, there were 72 pitchers on the IL with arm injuries. That figure jumped to 110 in 2020, a 53 percent increase.

There are a number of factors contributing to pitcher arm injuries, ranging from usage to velocity, but it appears that attenuated preseason training played a role. A lot of pitchers had super-short seasons due to arm woes. Corey Kluber, Roberto Osuna, and Shohei Ohtani combined for seven innings, none after August 8. All suffered arm injuries. We'll never know whether they'd have fared better with a longer preseason, but we can guess how they probably feel.

Everybody played.

Rosters were set to expand from 25 to 26 in 2020, so even if we'd had a normal season, we'd have likely seen 2019's record of 1,410 players on MLB rosters broken. But due to the pandemic, rosters started the year at 30 and were cut to only 28. Add multiple COVID-19 absences and the revolving door caused by poor starts by hitters and a rash of pitcher arm injuries, and 1,289 players appeared in MLB games in 2020. The comparable figure over the first 67 days of the 2019 season was 1,109. That 16 percent increase works out to an average of six more players per team in 2020 compared to a similar slice of 2019. A future look back at 2020 rosters will include a lot of unfamiliar names.

Plus became a minus.

In advanced metrics, we adjust batter and pitcher performance for park and league/era variations. A plus sign appended to the end of a measure means that it's adjusted for park and league. It's scaled to an average of 100, with higher figures above average and lower figures below average. (Similarly, a metric with a minus is also park- and league-adjusted and scaled to 100, with lower values better.) Here at BP, our advanced measure of offensive performance is DRC+. Baseball-Reference has OPS+ and FanGraphs has wRC+.

Using park and league adjustments, we can compare Dante Bichette's 1995 Steroid Era season at pre-humidor Coors Field (.340/.364/.620, 40 homers, 128 RBI, MVP runner-up) with Jim Wynn's 1968 Year of the Pitcher season at the cavernous Astrodome (.269/.376/.474, 26 homers, 67 RBI, no MVP votes). It's not close. DRC+, OPS+, and wRC+ all give the nod to Wynn, handily. This is a useful tool. As my Baseball Prospectus colleague Patrick Dubuque tweeted last fall, "Please note that when I ask how you are, I am already adjusting for era."

The 2020 season messes up plus (and minus) stats for two reasons. First, the park adjustment was based on only 30 home games instead of the usual 81. Everything noted above regarding the short season applies, literally doubly, to park effect calculations. DRC+ uses a single-season park factor. OPS+ uses a three-year average and wRC+ five years. The figure for 2020 is suspect.

Second, OPS+ and wRC+ adjust for league: American and National. (DRC+ adjusts for opponent, regardless of league.) While there were two leagues in 2020, they were an artificial construct. To reduce travel, teams played opponents geographically, not based on league. There weren't two leagues, American and National. There were three, Western, Central, and Eastern.

That makes a difference because teams in the same league played in different run-scoring environments. AL teams scored 4.58 runs per game, NL teams 4.71. That's a small difference. But teams in the East scored 0.21 more runs per game (4.95) than teams in the West (4.74), and they both scored a lot more than Central teams (4.25). Adjusting for league misses that difference, so this book will be safe in that regard, but other sources may be distorted somewhat.

Not every game was a "game."
In 2020, the rising tide of strikeouts was finally stemmed. Strikeouts per team per game fell from 8.8 in 2019 to 8.7 in 2020. That marked the first decline after 14 straight annual increases.

In 2020, the rising tide of strikeouts rose higher. Batters struck out in 23.4 percent of plate appearances compared to 23.0 percent in 2019. That marked the 15th straight annual increase.

Both are true statements.

Because of two rule changes—seven-inning doubleheaders and runners on second in extra innings—games in 2020 were unprecedented in their brevity. There were 37.0 plate appearances per game in 2020. The only years with fewer were 1904 and 1906-1909. The average game in 2020 entailed 8.61 innings pitched, the fewest since 1899.

So when you see any per-game stats for 2020, you need to increase them by 3 or 4 percent to get them on equal footing with recent years.

Or, better, just ignore them. Last year happened. There were major league games contested between major league teams. But when you're looking at those physical or electronic baseball cards, when you're weaving narratives over why this young player's inevitable rise to stardom fell apart or why that old veteran rekindled his magic, don't linger on the 2020 line. It was just too weird.

Thanks to Lucas Apostoleris for research assistance.

—*Rob Mains is an author of Baseball Prospectus.*

Tranches of WAR

by Russell A. Carleton

We ask "replacement level" to be a lot of things. Sometimes contradictory things. Sometimes I wonder if we know what it even means anymore. The original idea was that it represented the level of production that a team could expect to get from "freely available talent", including bench players, minor leaguers, and waiver wire pickups. It created a common benchmark to compare everyone to, and for that reason, it represented an advancement well beyond what was available at the time. In fact, it created a language and a framework for evaluating players that was not just better but *entirely* different than what came before it.

But then we started mumbling in that language. The idea behind "wins above replacement" was one part sci-fi episode and one part mathematical exercise. Imagine that a player had disappeared before the season and suddenly, in an alternate timeline, his team would have had to replace him. The distance between him and that replacement line was his value. We need to talk about that alternate timeline.

Without getting too into 2:00 am "deep conversations" with extensive navel-gazing, it's worth thinking about why one player might not be playing, while another might.

- A player might not be playing because he has a short-term injury or his manager believes that he needs a day off.
- A player might not be playing because he has a longer-term injury that requires him to be on the injured list.

There's a difference here between these two situations. In particular, the first one generally *doesn't* involve a compensatory roster move, while the second one does. It's possible, though not guaranteed, that the person who will be replacing the injured/resting player would be the same in either case. That matters. Teams generally carry a spare part for all eight position players on the diamond, although in the era of a four-player bench, those spare parts usually are the backup plan for more than one spot.

A couple of years ago, I posed a hypothetical question. Suppose that a team had two players in its system fighting for a fourth outfielder spot. One of them was a league average hitter, but would be worth 20 runs below average if allowed to play center field for a full season. One of them was a perfectly average fielder, but would be 15 runs below average as a hitter, if allowed to play an entire season. Which of the two should the team roster? It's tempting to say the second one, as overall, he is the better player. That misses the point. A league average hitter on the bench isn't just a potential replacement for an injured outfielder. He might also pinch hit for the light-hitting shortstop in a key spot. You keep the average hitter on the roster, even though he isn't a hand-in-glove fit for one specific place on the field, because being a bench player is a different job description than being a long-term fill-in for someone. If you find yourself in need of a longer-term fill-in, you can bring the other guy up from AAA.

When we're determining the value of an everyday player though, if he had disappeared before the season and a team would have had to replace his production, they likely would have done it with a player who was a long-term fill-in type because they would have had to replace a guy who played everyday. Maybe that's the same guy that they would have rostered on their bench anyway, but we don't know. It gets to the query of what we hope to accomplish with WAR. Are we looking for an accurate modeling of reality or are we looking for a common baseline to compare everyone to? Both have their uses, but they are somewhat different questions.

Let's talk about another dichotomy.

- A player might not be playing because he isn't very good and is a bench-level player.
- A player might not be playing because there is another player on the team who has a situational advantage that makes him the better choice today. The classic case of this is a handedness platoon. On another day, he might be a better choice.

When we think about player usage, I think we're still stuck in the model that there are starters and there are scrubs. We have plenty of words for bench players or reserves or backups or utility guys. We do still have the word "platoon" in our collective vocabulary, but in the age of short benches, it's hard to construct one. It's always been hard to construct them. You have to find two players who hit with different hands, have skill sets that complement each other, and probably play the same position. In the era of the short bench, one of them had probably better double as a utility player in some way. Baseball has a two-tiered language geared toward the idea of regulars and reserves. The fact that it was so easy for me to find plenty of synonyms for "a player whose primary function is to come into a game to replace a regular player if he is injured or resting" should tell you something.

I'm always one to look for "unspoken words" in baseball. What is it called when someone is both half of a platoon and the utility infielder? That guy exists sometimes, but he reveals himself in that role—usually by accident. We don't have a word for that, and whenever I find myself saying "we don't have a word for that", I look for new opportunities. What do you call it, further, when the job of being the utility infielder is decentralized across the whole infield with occasional contributions from the left fielder? It's not even a "super-utility" player. What happens when you build your entire roster around the idea that everyone will be expected to be a triple major?

⚾ ⚾ ⚾

I think someone else beat me to this one, and on a grand scale. Platoons work because we know that hitters of the opposite hand to the pitcher get better results than hitters of the same hand, usually to the tune of about 20 points of OBP. If you want to express that in runs, it usually comes out to somewhere around 10 to 12 runs of linear weights value prorated across 650 PA. But hang on a second, now let's say that we have two players who might start today, both of roughly equal merit with the bat. One has a handedness advantage, but is the worse fielder of the two. In that case, as long as his "over the course of a season" projection as a fielder at whatever position you want to slot him into is less than a 10-run drop from the guy he might replace, then he's a better option today.

We're not used to thinking of utility players as bat-first options, who would play below-average defense at three different infield positions. That guy might hook on as a 2B/3B/LF type (Howie Kendrick, come on down!) but teams usually think to themselves that they need as their utility infielder someone who "can handle" shortstop, the toughest of the infield spots to play. If someone can do that *and* hit well, he's probably already starting somewhere, so he's not available as a utility infielder. It's easier for those glove guys to find a job. In a world where the replacement for a shortstop *has to be* the designated utility infielder, that makes sense.

But as we talked about last week, we're living in a different world. The rate at which a replacement for a regular starter turns out to be *another starter* shifting over to cover has gone way up over the last five years. There was always some of it in the game, but this has been a supernova of switcheroos. Now if your second baseman is capable of playing a decent shortstop, that 2B/3B/LF guy can swap in. He's not actually playing shortstop, and maybe the defense suffers from the switch, but if he's got enough of a bat, he might outhit those extra fielding miscues. And in doing so, he is effectively your backup shortstop.

Somewhere along the lines, teams got hip to the idea of multi-positional play from their regulars. I've written before about how you can't just put a player, however athletic, into a new position and expect much at first. The data tell us that. Eventually, players can learn to be multi-positionalists, but it takes time, roughly on the order of two months, before they're OK. But there's a hidden message in there. If you give a player some reps at a new spot, he's a reasonably gifted athlete and somewhat smart and willing to learn, he could probably pick it up enough to get to "good enough," and it doesn't take forever. You just have to be purposeful about it. Maybe you get to the point where you can start to say "he's still below average but we could move him there and get another bat into the lineup, and it's a net win."

Teams have started to build those extra lessons into their player development program. It used to be seen as a mark of weakness to be relegated to "utility player" because that meant that you were a bench player (all those synonyms above come with a side of stigma). Now, it's a way of building a team. If you get a few reps in the minors (where it doesn't count) at a spot, you'll have at least played the spot at game speed before. There are limits to how far you can push that. A slow-footed "he's out in left field because we don't have the DH" guy is never going to play short, but maybe your third baseman can try second base and not look like a total moose out there.

⚾ ⚾ ⚾

Back to WAR. I'd argue that the world of starters and scrubs is slowly disintegrating, for good cause. In the event that a regular starter really does go down with an injury–ostensibly, the alternate universe scenario that WAR is attempting to model–it makes the team a little more resilient to replacing him. And the good news is that you're more likely to be able to replace him with the best of the bench bunch, rather than the third-best guy, because the best guy doesn't have to be an exact positional match for the guy who got hurt. And that's what the manager would want to do. He'd want to replace that long-term production, not with an amalgam of everyone else who played that position, but with the best guy available from his reserves.

Now this is still WAR. We still want to retain the principle that we should be measuring a player, and not his teammates. We need some sort of common baseline, and despite what I just said, we'll still need some sort of amalgam. To construct that, I give to you the idea of the tranche. The word, if you've not heard it before, refers to a piece of a whole that is somehow segmented off. It's often used in finance to talk about layers of a financial instrument.

Here, I want you to consider that there are 30 starters at each of the seven non-battery positions (catchers should have their own WAR, since only a catcher can replace a catcher). We can identify them by playing time, and we can futz around with the definition a little bit if we need to. Next, among those who aren't in that starting pool, we identify the top tranche of the 30 best bench players, which I would again identify by playing time, and then the second and third and fourth and so on. If a player were to disappear, his manager would probably want to take a guy from that top tranche of the bench to replace him. In a world where even the starters can slide around the field, that becomes more feasible.

We can take a look at that top tranche and say "How many of them showed that they are able to play (first, second, etc.)?" and therefore could have directly substituted for the starter? How many of them could have been a direct substitute for our injured player? We don't know whether one of them would be on *a specific* team, but we can say that 40 percent of the time, a manager would have been able to draw from tranche 1 in filling the role, and 35 percent from tranche 2. But on tranche 1, we can also look at how many of those players played a position that could have then shifted and covered for that spot. We'd need some eligibility criteria for all of this (probably a minimum number of games played) but it would just be a matter of multiplication. Shortstop would be harder to fill, and managers would probably be dipping a little further down in the talent pool, and so replacement level would be lower, as it is now.

Doing some quick analysis, I found that the difference in just batting linear weights (haven't even gotten into running or fielding) between tranche 1 and tranche 2 in 2019 was about 6.5 runs, prorated across 650 PA. Between tranche 1 and tranche 3, it's 10.8 runs. The ability to shift those plate appearances up the ladder has some real value.

This part is important. We can also give credit to starters for the positions that they showed an ability to play, even if they didn't play them (this is the guy fully capable of playing center, but who's in a corner because the team already has a good center fielder) because he allows a team to carry a player who hits like a left fielder to functionally be the team's backup center fielder. He facilitates that movement upward among the tranches. We can start to appreciate the difference between a left fielder who would never be able to hack it in center (and the compensatory move that his team would have to make) and the left fielder who could do it, but just didn't have to very often.

Past that, you can continue to use whatever hitting and fielding and running metrics you like to determine a player's value, but when we get down to constructing that baseline, I'd argue we need a better conceptual and mathematical framework. It's going to require some more #GoryMath than we're used to, but I'd argue it's a better conceptualization of the way that MLB actually plays the game in 2020. If…y'know…MLB plays in 2020. If WAR is going to be our flagship statistic among the *acronymati*, then we need to acknowledge that it contains some old and starting-to-be-out-of-date assumptions about the game. We may need to tinker with it. Here's my idea for how.

—Russell A. Carleton *is an author of Baseball Prospectus.*

Secondhand Sport

by Patrick Dubuque

Back before time stopped, I liked to go to thrift stores. Now that I'm older, I rarely ever buy anything—I don't need much in my life, now—but I still enjoy the old familiar circuit: check to see if there are baseball cards to write about, look for board or card games to play with the kids, scan for random ironic jerseys, hit the book section. It takes ten, maybe fifteen minutes. Thrift stores are the antithesis of modern online shopping, because you don't know what they have, and you don't even really know what you want. It's junk, literal junk, stuff other people thought was worthless. That's what makes it great.

In an idealized economy, thrift stores shouldn't exist. Everybody has a living wage, and every product has a durability that exactly matches its desired life; nothing should need to be given away, no one should need to be given to. But then, thrift stores shouldn't work on a customer experience level, either. You wouldn't think an ethos of "let's make everything disorganized and hard to find" would lead to customer satisfaction, but low-budget retailers like TJ Maxx and Ross thrive on this model. People like bargain hunting as much for the hunting as the bargain; it's part of the experience, spending time as if it's a wager. There's a thrill, occasionally, in inefficiency.

In sports, the modern overuse of the word "inefficiency" is a condemnation: It insinuates that there is *an* efficiency, a correct way to be found, and that all other ways are wrong ways. It's prevalent in baseball but hardly contained to it; the lifehack, the Silicon Valley disruption are other examples of productivity creep in our daily lives. Their modern success makes plenty of sense. Maximization of resources, after all, is its own puzzle, and an industry of European board games is founded upon it. It's fun to take a system and optimize it, unravel it like a sudoku puzzle. If there's only one kind of genius, after all, there's no way anyone can fail to appreciate it.

Baseball has been hacking away at these perceived inefficiencies since its inception: platoons, bullpens, farm systems were all installed to extract more out of the tools at hand. But it's been a particular badge of the sabermetric movement, from Ken Phelps and his All-Star Team to Ricardo Rincon and the darlings of *Moneyball*. It's business, but it's also an ethos: the idea that there's treasure among the trash, something we all failed to appreciate until someone brought it to light.

It's the myth that made Sidd Finch so enticing, that fuels so many "best shape" narratives and new pitch promises. We all, athletes and unathletic sportswriters, want to believe that there's genius trapped inside us, and that it's just a matter of puzzling out the combination to unlock it. That our art, our style is the next inefficiency, waiting for our own Billy Beane. It's why we root for underdogs, and why we're excited for the Mike Tauchmans and the Eurubiel Durazos, champions of skin-deep mediocrity.

Except we aren't anymore, really. The days of "Free X" have descended beyond the ring of irony and into obscurity. There are still Xs to be freed, or at least one X, duplicated endlessly: Mike Ford, Luke Voit, Max Muncy. The undervalued one-dimensional slugger demonstrated how the game hasn't quite culturally caught up to its logical extreme. But for those who don't fit the rather spacious mold, times are grimmer. As Rob Arthur revealed several months ago, there's been a marked increase in the number of sub-replacement relievers. It's the outcome of a greater number of teams forced to play out games without the talent to win them, but it's also emblematic of the modern tendency of teams to dispose of their disposable assets, burning through cost-controlled arms the way that man chopped down forests in *The Lorax*. Stuff just isn't built to outlive their original owners anymore.

It's unsurprising, given how well-mined the market for inefficiencies has been of late. The disciples of the early analytics departments, and the disciples of those, have proliferated the league, with only a few backwater holdouts. The league has grown smarter, but every team has learned the same lesson. In fact, the phenomenon creates a peculiar kind of feedback loop: As teams value a specific subset of players or skills, prospective athletes learn to increase their own marketability by conforming themselves to the demands of their prospective employers.

And that's tragic, in the way that the extinction of animals is tragic; a certain amount of biodiversity in baseball has been lost. Shortstops hit like outfielders. Pitchers don't hit at all. Only the catchers remain idiosyncratic, thanks to the defensive demands of their position; eventually they too will be required to produce like everyone else, or they'll meet the fate of their battery mates. A perfect economy requires perfect production.

I mentioned earlier that more and more, I leave thrift stores empty-handed. It is true that I am more discerning than in the past; my bookshelves are full, and there are more streaming films than I will ever be able to watch. But there are other factors at play.

Thrift stores are, in a way, the bond markets of retail. When the economy is rough and other retailers are struggling, more people look secondhand for their products. But as recently as last year, publications were noting a reversal of the trend: Companies like Goodwill and Savers were expanding despite a strong economy. Publications credited a heightened sense of environmentalism and a rejection of cutting-edge fashion as drivers behind the increase, though the more likely answer is the modern American economy hasn't showered its favors equally, particularly among the young.

But it is more than just the economy. Baseball and thrift stores share something else in common, evident in our current conversations about re-starting the sport: They live in the gray area between public service and private enterprise. Thrift stores provide affordable necessities to lower-class citizens, and collectibles and fashion for the middle-class. Because of the success of the latter, prices have gone up across the board. Especially in terms of clothing, the middle-class flight from fashion into vintage has instead carried the aftereffects of fashion, including its costs, into a territory where people just want clothes. But there's another factor in the rise of prices, in the form of the internet.

The Goodwills of the world have grown smarter, too, employing the internet to extract full value from their detritus. Ebay, similarly, has lost much of the charm it had as a new frontier around the turn of the century. Everything has a price point now; even individual taste is no match for the algorithm, because anything rare, no matter how niche its market, is a collectible to someone.

The internet has had the same effect on thrift stores that sabermetrics has had on baseball; its equivalent to OBP was the bar scanner. As detailed in Slate, the rise of second-party stores on eBay and Amazon birthed an entire industry of used-good salespeople, armed with PDAs and scanners, buying books for three dollars to sell online for five. The author, Michael Savitz, reports earning $60,000 by working nearly 80 hours a week; he makes it clear that this is not a vocation of his choosing. It's long hours, with no real creativity or individuality, skimming the cream off of a local establishment and flipping it to someone with a little more money on the other side of the country. And once the vocation exists, the obvious question arises: why wait to put the wares out on the shelves? Why allow value to exist at all?

Nothing is ruined. Thrift stores will continue to sell polo shirts and DVDs, and baseball will continue to exist and make or lose money, depending on who you believe. But as we continue to refine our knowledge, we lose something in the conquest for efficiency, a delight born out of the unknown. The problem isn't the efficiency itself; we can't blame the booksellers, or the people sweeping freeways to collect grams of platinum from damaged catalytic converters. The problem is a system that requires this sort of profit-skimming behavior in order to feed families (or, for corporations, maximize shareholder return).

Arizona Diamondbacks 2021

In times like these, with the 2020 season on the brink and the collective bargaining agreement close behind, it can often feel like the current situation is untenable. It can't keep going like this, even if we don't know what to do about it. But as with thrift stores, there's an equally irresistible feeling that it *has* to keep going, that it would be unimaginable to not have this broken, amazing sport. Both industries exist on an invisible foundation of friction, of chaos and unpredictability, even as both see their foundations buffed down to a perfect, untouchable polish. But if COVID-19 and its financial ramifications do, as some have suggested, make it such that the baseball that returns is fundamentally different than the baseball that came before, perhaps this is the time to lean in, and change the game even more. Fix bunting. Make defense more difficult. Create viable, alternate strategies. Add some chaos back into baseball. It's fun when no one knows quite where things are.

—*Patrick Dubuque is an author of Baseball Prospectus.*

Steve Dalkowski Dreaming

by Steven Goldman

We dream of being a pitcher, of starring in the major leagues. Depending on your age and your sense of historical perspective, you might imagine yourself as Walter Johnson, throwing harder than anyone else—hitting more batters than anyone else, too, but always feeling bad about it. You could picture yourself as a Tom Seaver or a David Cone, with all the stuff in the world but still being cerebral about it, thinking about so much more than burning 'em in there. There are so many models one could choose: You could be a Lefty Gomez, Jim Bouton, or Bill Lee, skilled, but not taking the whole thing too seriously, or a Lefty Grove, Bob Gibson, or Steve Carlton, powerful but treating each start like a mission to be survived instead of a game to be enjoyed.

Very few would dream of being Steve Dalkowski, the former Baltimore Orioles prospect who died of COVID-19 last week at the age of 80. Yet, there is something just as noble in Dalkowski's negative accomplishments—and accomplishments is what they are—as there is in the precision-engineered pitching of a Greg Maddux. You have to be very good to be that bad. Dalkowski had all of the stuff of the greatest pitchers but none of the command; his story is not one of failing to conquer his limitations, but striving against one of the cruelest hands that fate or genetics or personality can deal us: A desire to achieve great things which is almost but not quite matched by the ability to meet that goal.

As with Johnson, Grove, Bob Feller, and the rest of the hard-throwing pitchers who played before the advent of modern radar guns, we have to take the word of the players and coaches who saw Dalkowski pitch as to his velocity. He was a hard-drinking, maximum-effort pitcher who, if their memories are to be believed, consistently threw over 100 miles per hour. His was the Maltese Fastball, the stuff that dreams are made of. The problem is that velocity without command and control is still a good distance from utility. Dalkowski was the most effective towel you could design for a fish, the sleekest bathing suit intended to be worn by an astronaut, but that doesn't mean he wasn't beautiful: We can appreciate a journey even if it doesn't end at the intended destination.

Whether because of sloppy mechanics he couldn't calm, an inability to understand that a consistent 98 in the strike zone would likely be more effective than a consistent 110 out of it, or all that beer, Dalkowski could never make the adjustments that pitchers like Feller and Nolan Ryan made before him, possibly because he had so far to go: Feller, who never pitched in the minors, came up at 17 and spent three years walking almost seven batters per nine innings before settling in at 3.8 beginning when he was 20. Ryan started out walking over six batters per nine but gradually improved as his long career played out; for him to go from 6.2 walks per nine with the 1966 Greenville Mets to 3.7 with the 1989 Texas Rangers represents a 40 percent reduction. An equivalent improvement by Dalkowski would still have left him walking over 11 batters per nine innings.

Dalkowski was like *The Room* of pitchers, a player so bad he became good again. Cal Ripken, Sr., who both played with and managed Dalkowski, recalled in a 1979 *Sporting News* "where are they now" piece the occasion when the pitcher crossed up his catcher and his fastball, "hit the plate umpire smack in the mask. The mask broke all to pieces and the umpire wound up in the hospital for three days with a concussion. If they ever had a radar gun in those days, I'll bet Dalkowski would have been timed at 110 miles an hour."

Signed by the Orioles out of New Britain High in Connecticut in 1957, Dalkowski was sent to Kingsport in the Appalachian League, where he pitched 62 innings. He allowed only 22 hits in 62 innings, or 3.2 per nine, a number with no equivalent in major league history (though Aroldis Chapman came close in 2014), and also struck out 121 (17.6 per nine) and walked 129 (18.7). He was also charged with 39 wild pitches. That June, one of his fastballs clipped a Dodgers prospect named Bob Beavers and carried away part of his ear. "The first pitch was over the backstop, the second pitch was called a strike, I didn't think it was," Beavers said last year. "The third pitch hit me and knocked me out, so I don't remember much after that. I couldn't get in the sun for a while, and I never did play baseball again." Former minor leaguer Ron Shelton based the *Bull Durham* pitcher Nuke LaLoosh on Dalkowski. And yet, to see him as a figure of fun, an amusing loser, is to misunderstand something unique and strange.

Dalkowski kept on posting some of the strangest lines in baseball history. Pitching for the Stockton Ports of the Class C California League in 1960, he struck out 262 and walked 262 in 170 innings. Yet, he did improve, especially after pitching for Earl Weaver at Elmira in 1962. Weaver had previously had Dalkowski at Aberdeen in 1959, but wasn't ready to grapple with him then. This time he was. "I had grown more and more concerned about players with great physical abilities who could not learn to correct certain basic deficiencies no matter how much you instructed or drilled them," he related in his autobiography, *It's What You Learn After You Know It All That Counts*. He got permission from the Orioles to give all of his players the Stanford-Binet IQ test. "Dalkowski finished in the 1 percentile in his ability to understand facts. Steve, it was said to say, had the ability to do everything but learn." [sic]

IQ tests are problematic diagnostic tools, so take Weaver's estimate of Dalkowski's mental capabilities with a grain of salt. What's important is that even if he got to the right answer by way of the wrong reason, Weaver had learned something valuable. His insight was to stop asking Dalkowski to learn new pitches and just let him get by with the two that he had. Were Dalkowski a prospect today, that would have been a no-brainer: Can't develop a third pitch? The bullpen is right over there, sir. Player development wasn't like that then, but Weaver, temporarily Dalkowski's mentor, could let him work with what he had. According to Weaver, the pitcher responded: "In the final 57 innings he pitched that season Dalkowski gave up 1 earned run, struck out 110 batters, and walked only 11." It's not true—as per the *Elmira Star-Gazette*, as of late July, Dalkowski had walked 71 in 106 innings and finished with 114 in 160 innings, which means Dalkowski's control actually faded at the end of the season rather than improved—but that doesn't mean it didn't happen in some sense, just that it didn't happen that way. Again, it's the journey, not the destination, and his ERA was 3.04 so *something* had gone right.

Also along the way: The next spring, Orioles manager Billy Hitchcock was rooting for Dalkowski to make the team as a long-man—maybe Weaver had gotten through to him. There were things out of Weaver's control, like the universe's twisted sense of humor: that March, Dalkowski's elbow went "twang."

You sometimes read that it was the Orioles' insistence on Dalkowski learning the curve that did him in, but even if they hadn't learned their lesson, the injury was probably just a coincidence: Dalkowski had thrown an incredible number of pitches over the previous few years. Still, it testifies to the dangers of trying to get what you want and risking the loss of what you had. Dalkowski tried to come back, but the 110-mph stuff was gone. A pitcher with no control and no stuff is…a civilian. What followed were years of vagabond living, arrests for drunkenness. There were Alcoholics Anonymous meetings, assistance from baseball alumni associations, but none of it took. From the 1990s until the time of his passing he dwelt in an assisted living facility, suffering from alcohol-related dementia. He'd been a heavy drinker since his teenage years. As with all those pitches per game, there was a price to be paid. You make choices on the journey and some of them are irrevocable. It's like a fairy tale: "Bite of poison apple? Don't mind if I do."

In the aforementioned *Sporting News* profile, Chuck Stevens, the head of the Association of Professional Ballplayers of America, a ballplayer charity, said, "I've got nothing against drinking. I do it myself sometimes. But, I don't condone common drunkenness. We went through lots of heartache and many dollars, but Dalkowski didn't want to help himself and we weren't going to keep him drunk." The journey is *un*like a fairy tale: No one will come along and kiss it better, not if they're busy forming judgments.

In the end, we are left with a sort of philosophical chicken/egg conundrum: Is failing to meet your goals evidence of unfulfilled potential or the lack of it? Isn't what you did by definition what you were capable of doing? Or could you have broken through to something better with the right help, the right lucky break? These are unanswerable questions, and how we try to answer them may say more about us than about the people we're judging.

No pitcher ever has it easy. *All* pitchers must work hard. *All* pitchers must refine their craft. It's almost never just about *stuff*. Dalkowski dreaming is no insult to the great pitchers who made it; from Pete Alexander to Max Scherzer, they have all earned their way up. And yet, if it is true that we can only do as much as we can do, then the journey would be more of an adventure, the ultimate triumph or defeat more noble, if like Dalkowski we lacked 100 percent of the confidence, the command, the self-possession, the commitment, the resistance to making bad decisions that so many great players possess—to be gloriously human. Or, to put it more succinctly, it would be fun to be able to throw as hard as any person ever has. Even if just for a moment, and even if nothing more came of it than that, no one could say you hadn't lived life to the fullest.

—Steven Goldman is an author of Baseball Prospectus.

A Reward For A Functioning Society

by Cory Frontin and Craig Goldstein

On July 5, Nationals reliever Sean Doolittle said in the middle of a press conference regarding the restart of Major League Baseball and what would later be known as summer camp, "sports are like the reward of a functioning society." This sentence was amidst a much longer, thoughtful reply about the societal and health conditions under which MLB players were being brought back. It's a very similar sentiment to one Jane McManus used on April 7, when she discussed the White House's meeting with sports commissioners. She said "sports are the effect of a functioning society—not the precursor."

Both versions of the same sentiment spoke to a laudable ideal in the context of a country that was not addressing a rampaging virus, and opting instead to bring sports back for the feeling of normalcy rather than the reality of it. "Priorities," as McManus said.

On Wednesday, the NBA's Milwaukee Bucks conducted a wildcat/political strike, refusing to come out for Game 5 of their playoff series against the Orlando Magic. The Magic refused to accept the forfeit, and shortly thereafter other playoff series were threatened by player strikes. Eventually the league moved to postpone that day's games, folding to players leveraging their united power.

The backdrop against which these actions took place was the shooting by police of Jacob Blake. Blake was shot in the back seven times by police, as he attempted to get into his vehicle. He managed to survive the assault, but is paralyzed from the waist down.

⚾ ⚾ ⚾

The step taken to walk out, first by the Milwaukee Bucks, then subsequently by other NBA, WNBA, and MLB teams, was a step toward upholding the virtue of the sentiment described by McManus and Doolittle. But that sentiment does not align with the broad history of sports in this and other countries, a history that contradicts the core of the idealistic statement.

Sports have been a significant part of American society for most of its existence, expanding in importance and influence in recent years. The idea that society was functioning in a way that was worthy of the reward of sports for most of that time is laughable. Much of America is not functioning and has not functioned for Black people, full stop. The oppressed people at the center of this political act by players, specifically Black players, in concert throughout the NBA and in fits and starts throughout Major League Baseball, have not known a society that functions for them rather than *because* of them.

Politics has been part of the sports landscape since the inception of sport, but for just about as long people have bemoaned its presence. Sports are to be an escape, it is said. An escape from what, though? A functioning society?

No, the presence of sports has never signified a cultural or political system that is on the up and up. Rather, the presence of sports *reflect and reinforce the society that produces them.*

⚾   ⚾   ⚾

The Negro Leagues were born out of societal dysfunction. The need for entirely separate leagues, composed of Black and Latino players barred from the Major Leagues because of racism? That is not a functioning society, and yet there were sports.

Even the integration of players from the Negro Leagues resulted in a transfer of power and wealth from Black-owned businesses and communities and into white ones, mirroring the dysfunction that had bled into every aspect of American society at the time. Japheth Knopp noted in the Spring 2016 Baseball Research Journal:

> *The manner in which integration in baseball—and in American businesses generally—occurred was not the only model which was possible. It was likely not even the best approach available, but rather served the needs of those in already privileged positions who were able to control not only the manner in which desegregation occurred, but the public perception of it as well in order to exploit the situation for financial gain. Indeed, the very word integration may not be the most applicable in this context because what actually transpired was not so much the fair and equitable combination of two subcultures into one equal and more homogenous group, but rather the reluctant allowance—under certain preconditions—for African Americans to be assimilated into white society.*

To understand the value of a movement, though, is not to understand how it is co-opted by ownership, but to know the people it brings together and what they demand. When Jackie Robinson—the player who demarcated the inevitability of the end of the Negro leagues—attended the March on Washington for Jobs and Freedom in 1963, he did so with his family and marched alongside the people. He stood alongside hundreds of thousands to fight for their common civil and labor rights. "The moral arc of the universe is long," many freedom fighters have echoed, "but it bends towards justice." The bend, it is less frequently said, happens when a great mass of people place the moral arc of the universe on their knee and apply force, as Jackie, his family, and thousands of others did that day.

⚾ ⚾ ⚾

Of course, taking the moral arc of the universe down from the mantle and bending it is not without risk. Perhaps the outsized influence of athletes is itself a mark of a dysfunctional society, but, nonetheless, hundreds of athletes woke up on Wednesday morning with the power to bring in millions of dollars in revenues. That very power, as we would come to find out, was matched with the equal and opposite power to *not* bring those revenues. That power, in hands ranging from the Milwaukee Bucks, to Kenny Smith in the *Inside the NBA* Studio, from the unexpected ally, Josh Hader, and his largely white teammates to the notably Black Seattle Mariners, would be exercised for a single demand: the end to state violence against Black people. Not unlike the March itself, it sat at the intersection of the civil rights of Black Americans and bold labor action. The March on Washington stood in the face of a false notion of integration—against an integration of extraction but not one of equality—and proposed something different. Just the same, the acts of solidarity of August 26, 2020 will be remembered in stark defiance of MLB's BLM-branded, but ultimately empty displays on opening weekend.

Bold defiance like this can never be without risk. By choosing to exercise this power, the Milwaukee Bucks took a risk. They risked vitriol and backlash from those they disagreed with. They risked fines or seeing their contracts voided, as a walkout like this is prohibited by their CBA. They risked forfeiting a playoff game, one that, as the No. 1 seed in the playoffs, they'd worked all year to attain. They didn't know how Orlando would respond. It wasn't clear that other teams throughout the league would follow suit in solidarity. And it wasn't known the league would accept these actions and moderately co-opt them by "postponing" games that would have featured no players.

If the league reschedules the games, some of the athletes' risk—their shared sacrifice—will be diminished, in retrospect. But they did not know any of that when they took that risk. And it is often left to athletes to take these risks when others in society won't, especially those of their same socioeconomic status and levels of influence.

It is athletes, specifically BIPOC athletes, that take them, though, because they live with the risk of being something other than white in this country every day. They are no strangers to the realities of police brutality. It seems incongruous then, to say that sports are a reward for a functioning society when we rely on athletes to lead us closer to being a functioning society. Luckily, our beloved athletes, WNBA players first and foremost among them, understand what sports truly are: a pipebender for the moral arc of the universe.

—Craig Goldstein is editor in chief of Baseball Prospectus. Cory Frontin is an author of Baseball Prospectus.

Index of Names

Ahmed, Nick 16
Beasley, Jeremy 80
Beer, Seth 68, 93
Bergen, Travis 36
Bukauskas, J.B. 80, 95
Bumgarner, Madison 38
Calhoun, Kole 18
Carroll, Corbin 69, 88
Castellanos, Humberto 40
Cecconi, Slade 81, 92
Clarke, Taylor 42
Crichton, Stefan 44
Cron, Kevin 70
Devenski, Chris 81
Duplantier, Jon 82, 95
Escobar, Eduardo 20
Espinal, Jeferson 95
Fairchild, Stuart 95
Fletcher, Dominic 95
Frias, Luis 94
Gallen, Zac 46
Ginkel, Kevin 48
Henry, Tommy 94
Jarvis, Bryce 83, 90
Jay, Jon 71
Jones, Adam 72
Kelly, Carson 22
Kelly, Levi 83, 93
Kelly, Merrill 50
Leake, Mike 84
Leyba, Domingo 72
Locastro, Tim 24
López, Yoan 52
Marte, Ketel 26
Martin, Corbin 84, 91
Mathisen, Wyatt 73
Mejia, Humberto 54, 96
Mella, Keury 85
Patino, Wilderd 94
Peralta, David 28
Perdomo, Geraldo 74, 89
Robinson, Kristian 75, 87
Rojas, Josh 30
Smith, Caleb 56
Smith, Pavin 76, 95
Smith, Riley 58
Soria, Joakim 60
Thomas, Alek 76, 88
VanMeter, Josh 77
Varsho, Daulton 32
Vogt, Stephen 78
Walker, Christian 34
Walston, Blake 86, 91
Weaver, Luke 62
Widener, Taylor 64, 96
Young, Alex 66
Young, Andy 79

For the Joy of Keeping Score

THIRTY81 Project is an ongoing graphic design project focused on the ballparks of baseball. Since being established in 2013, scorecards have been a fundemantal part of the effort. Each two-page card is uniquely ballpark-centric — there are 30 variants — and designed with both beginning and veteran scorekeepers in mind. Evolving over the years with suggestions from fans, broadcasters, and official scorers, the sheets are freely available to everyone as printable letter-size PDFs at the project webshop: www.THIRTY81Project.com

Download, Print, Score, Repeat ...

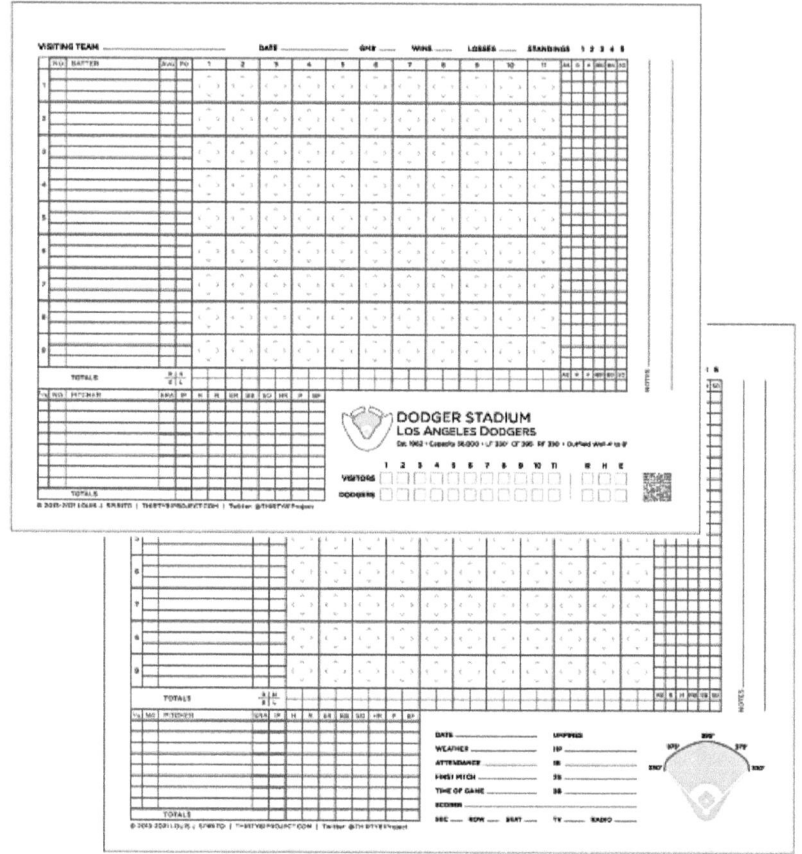

Scorecard design ©2013-2021 Louis J. Spirito | THIRTY81Project